© 2020 Anima Mundi Publishing

Ask and Receive
By:
Zim van Dijk

All rights reserved. No part of this publication may be reproduced, stored in a retrieval system or transmited in any form or by any means, electronic, mechanical, photocopying, recording or otherwise without the prior permision of the publisher or in accordance with the provisions of the Copyright, Designs and Patents Act 1988 or under the terms of any licence permitting limited copying issued by the Copyright Licensing Angency.

Published by: Anima Mundi Publishing Corp
Interior and Cover Design by Arty Design

ISBN: 978-1-7363763-1-7

Printed in the United-States

Zim van Dijk

ASK and RECEIVE

The 7 Biblical Laws of Supplication

Ignore Them and Bear the Consequences

Anima Mundi Publishing Corp

"Ask, and it shall be given you"
(Mt 7:7, Lk 11:9)

"Ye ask, and receive not, because ye ask amiss"
(Jas 4:3)

Contents

Introduction 7
    The Promise 8
    The Source of Life 9
    The Iceman Cometh 13
    Prayer vs. Supplication 15

Law # 1

The Law of Invocation 19
    Your First Supplication 19
    To Whom Must Supplications Be Made? 24
    Idolaters, Ventriloquists and False Prophets 26
    Are intercessors needed? 33
    Is it OK to try anyway? 34
    What If I Err in Good Faith? 34
    Intercession of Saints and Angels 34
    Invoking Mary, Mother of Christ? 36
    Calling Upon the Name of Christ? 37
    Can We Call Upon the Holy Spirit? 38
    Calling Upon a Beloved Departed 39
    What did Augustine Think? 41
    What did Thomas Aquinas Think? 41
    Why do we have to Ask God? 41
    What Does the Scripture Say? 43

Law #2

The Law of God's Will 47

    Understanding the Will of God 47

    Who Can Teach What God's Will Is? 51

    Your Personal Quest for God 52

    God Is Immutable 53

    The Scripture, Word of God 54

    Why is God's Will Not In Writing? 56

    Understanding God's Will Through Observation 57

    Ask the Beasts, the Birds of the Sky 58

    What is Divine Providence? 65

    How Does Divine Providence Work? 67

    Confirmation by the Spirit 68

Law #3

The Law of Sanctification 71

    Holiness and Sanctification 71

    The Holiness Requirement 74

    How to Become Holy 77

    The First Commandment 79

    The Divine Grace 80

    What Does "In His Image" Mean? 81

    Sanctification Through Imitation 82

    Where to Start 82

    The Golden Rule 86

    The Royal Law 87

    See Yourself as God Sees You 93

    Listen to Your Inner Voice 94

    The Heavenly Cord 98

    Talking with God 100

Law #4
The Law of Ends & Means 103
- You don't know how to ask 103
- How Should You Ask? 105
- Behold the Newborn 108
- What Can You Ask? 110
- Agur's Supplication 113
- Solomon's Supplication 115
- Hezekiah's Supplication 116
- Why Is this Supplication So Noteworthy? 116
- What Did Hezekiah Receive? 118
- What did Socrates Say? 119
- What Did the Apostles Say? 120
- What Did Christ Say? 121
- Greatest Supplications of the Bible 123
- What Should You Not Ask? 124
- God's Privileges 125
- What Should you Absolutely Ask? 127
- To Be or Not to Be Heard? 130
- Summary 133

Law #5
The Law of Gratitude 137
- The Power of Alleluia 137
- Thank You O Lord My God 139
- When Should You Praise the Lord? 141
- Don't Go to God Empty-Handed 143
- The Power of Chanting 143
- Praise and Thanksgiving 146

Offerings and Sacrifices 147

A Gift from God 152

Joy and Happiness 152

Law #6

The Law of Elevation 155

What Does Elevation Mean? 155

Job's Trying Ordeal 156

Your Jacob's Ladder 158

Knowing Good and Evil 159

The Sprinter 163

The Noises 165

Fearing God 167

Being Heard by God 168

Spiritual Convergence 170

Self-effacement and Surrender 176

The Image of the Glory of God 179

How to Know God Is Talking to You? 183

The Language of God 185

How Did God Speak to the Prophets? 187

How God Speaks to Man Nowadays 191

Listening to God 198

Law #7

The Law of Consequences 203

What Does Consequence Mean? 203

Cause & Effect 206

Acts and Consequences 207

Motivation—Volition—Intention 207

Other People's Deeds? 209

Salvation and Eternal Life 210

Being Heard of God 211

Not Being Heard by God	213
Renouncing God's Forgiveness	213
Renouncing God's Grace	214
Forgoing God's Love	216
Moving God's Mercy Away from You	216
Wounds, Aches, and Afflictions	220
Saying "No" to the Divine Promise	221
Good Riddance to Providence	223
Being Forgotten by God	227
Salvation or Perdition	230
The Pit You Dug	231
Forgoing an Encounter with God	234
The Empty House	235
The Parable of the Empty House	236
Leave Not Your Mind Lie Fallow	237
The Fruit of the Spirit	239
The Word and the Spirit	239

Introduction

Supplication plays a fundamental role in Christian spirituality, yet it is poorly understood. Supplication is the surest way to obtain God's help, as explained in the scriptures. Through supplication, the soul of the supplicant ascends toward God, enters into intimate communication with Him, expresses its feelings of love and gratitude, and exposes its miseries and its wants. The Scripture says that if our prayers are unanswered, it's because we do not know how to ask. And yet, the Scripture tells us precisely and accurately what the immutable biblical laws of Supplication are. It is why I undertook this substantial study of the immutable laws of Supplication, according to the Bible. Without ignoring the hieratic character of the subject, I endeavored to study it from the standpoint of spirituality, and when I was writing, I let the divine word guide my pen. I was not writing with any future reader in mind; God was my sole audience. My goal was not to unduly influence or distract anyone from their beliefs or the traditions or practices of their church.

My only recommendation for those who desire to involve themselves in the study of the Scriptures is to do so with critical intelligence and an open mind. The Scripture teaches us to rid ourselves of conventional wisdom and use our intelligence to think differently, for this is how we come to discern good from evil and to understand what the divine will is. "Be not conformed to this world: but be ye transformed by the renewing of your mind, that ye may prove what is that good, and acceptable, and perfect, will of God." (Rom 12:2)

The Scripture reveals seven immutable laws of Supplication. Abide by them, and observe as your life changes forever; ignore them and accept the consequences.

The Promise

This guide is entirely dedicated to the divine promise, "Ask, and it shall be given you" (Mt 7:7, Lk 11:9), for the hope of this promise procures the strength to go through life and overcome its many hardships; and it is the assurance that the fruit of the Promise is always there for us to reclaim that which brings us peace of heart.

Life must be imbued with meaning and have a definite purpose to be worth living. Through the study of the Scriptures, you'll understand the meaning and purpose of your life. But let's be clear, to study the Scriptures in-depth, your whole life won't be enough. Why reinvent the wheel when thousands of wise men before us have mapped out the road for us?

This path opened by the elders is the only one we can take with confidence. The Hebrew people were the first to walk it, led by Abraham, the "father of believers," who serves as a model to all believers of today and tomorrow, according to the Bible. "He staggered not at the promise of God through unbelief; but was strong in faith, giving glory to God; And being fully persuaded that, what he had promised, he was able also to perform." (Rom 4:20–21).

Of all the mighty empires that dominated the world in the time of the Bible, Pharaohs' Egypt, Greece, the Roman Empire, the Byzantines, the Assyrians, Babylon, Sumer, the Persians, etc., none survived to this day; they all vanished. No other people endured so much hardship and adversity, yet the chosen people survived, and prosper in the land God had promised to Abraham.

We do not intend to immerse you deeply in an esoteric and complex study of the Scripture. Whether you are a novice or a learned reader of the Scriptures, you will need a little help to open your mind to the influence of the Word of God. We all need it. One purpose of this guide is to make you realize how the wisdom embodied in the Scripture can enhance your daily life. As for those who prefer to renounce this journey, alas, they will never know the happiness and fullness felt by those who have come closer to God to the point of perceiving His presence and the warmth of His breath.

This study of the seven immutable and eternal laws of Supplication according to the Bible, will accompany you throughout your spiritual journey to meet God and bring you some solid spiritual nourishment that will sustain you in your quest for God.

God is waiting for you, and He hopes He will see you come to Him. His arms are wide open for you. I say that because I met Him and since, my life has changed. Every day I live is the best day of my life, and those who follow Him will even be more beautiful. God has entered my life, and He dwells in me. Like David, God is my strength and my shield; my refuge and my savior; and I owe Him everything that I am today. Every day, in my prayers, I thank the Lord, for He made me who I am.

The Source of Life

The Bible contains the story of the chosen people and their relationship with God. The period covered by the Old Testament goes from the creation of the world and continues for several millennia. Before being written, the Old Testament was transmitted from generation to generation through oral tradition. The New Testament covers a period of about 70 to 90 years and bears witness to the life and teachings of Christ.

During the biblical period, including the apostolic era, the Pentateuch, the Law or the Torah of the Jews, which encompasses the first five books of the Bible (Genesis, Exodus, Leviticus, Numbers, and Deuteronomy) was the supreme authority, that is the Scripture. So, when Paul, Matthew, Mark, Luke, and John mention the Scripture, they refer to the Old Testament and mostly to the Pentateuch. The same is true of the quotations of Jesus Christ revealed in the New Testament. Christ knew by heart the complete text of the Old Testament and especially the Pentateuch, before his bar mitzvah at twelve. In the apostolic times, the Gospel did not exist yet. Paul died in AD 64–67, and the authors of the Gospel wrote it in AD 66–110.

I often hear that, to read the Bible you have to start with the New Testament and that understanding the Old Testament is optional, if not useless, and that if anyone is interested in the Old Testament texts, he should read through the books of Psalms and Proverbs and perhaps Isaiah's, and that will be enough. It is wrong! A Christian must strive to imitate Christ in his daily life and in every attempt at developing his spirituality. Christ knew the Old Testament by heart; the Jewish Bible was his only source. Thus, to imitate Christ, one must begin with reading the Old Testament, which Christians share with their elder brothers, the Jews. To better understand the teachings of Christ, one must drink from the same sources.

There are dozens of English translations of the Bible and each religion of The Book has a version of their own. Each denomination uses a translation they prefer, which sometimes contains significant differences with others. We can't help asking ourselves relevant questions. All descendants of Abraham, for instance, agree there is only one God; so there should logically be only one Bible for all. God did not inspire many prophets with different and contradictory thoughts. But the hand of man, alas, did its work. Good faith translators have made mistakes; audacious correctors have changed the meaning of a verse by preferring one word to another; no counting the hand of the scribe who, here and there, ventured to modify the word of God to favor the doctrine of his camp.

Thanks to your critical spirit and your intelligence, and with God's help, you will separate the wheat from the chaff and repair the outrage done to the Holy Word.

Rather than make an exhaustive inventory of the many ways to enter the Bible, I prefer to share my approach and leave you free to find yours. My favorite Bible lodged prominently on a shelf in my library, which it rarely left. A thousand times, though, I had asked myself the same question, "how to enter the Bible?" I was ashamed, I admit, to let the Holy Book amass dust in this role of figuration.

What kept me from taking The Book and read it was that I could not imagine how the men who lived in those days looked. Popular imagery depicts them with long beards and looking like patriarchs. I imagined them closer to Homo-Sapiens, Cro-Magnons, or Neanderthals, not the people I would socialize with and converse with, sipping a beer.

Moreover, having to delve into ancient comments, biblical analysis, discussions, and debates on the original texts and the accuracy of the translations, on the authenticity of the originals, on the numerous schools of thought and exegetical studies, did not encourage me.

Reading a good book on the subject, which would have brought me enough knowledge a teenager could have been contented with, did not tempt me. Today, there are books for everything, to learn how to breathe, to live, to make pastries, Chinese dishes, intelligent children, complicated trades and even simple trades,

Ignore them and bear the consequences

but nothing that could motivate me.

"This book of the law shall not depart out of thy mouth; but thou shalt meditate therein day and night, that thou mayest observe to do according to all that is written therein: for then thou shalt make thy way prosperous, and then thou shalt have good success." (Jo 1:8)

Entering the Bible is a laudable ambition, but where should you begin? Many Scripture learning candidates are discouraged by the sheer size of the Bible, and they postpone their plans because they do not know where to begin.

Many want to become familiar with the Bible and know the messages that God has given us, but they give up when confronted with the apparent difficulty of the task. Almost everyone has at least one Bible on their bookshelves, but how many have read it? How many have read at least a few paragraphs or even just a few verses? How many have read it outside their church? How many have studied it at least partially?

Some are legitimately intimidated by the magnitude of the task or the number of pages to read. Who has ever read a book of over 1000 pages as imposing as the Bible? Others are hesitant, because of ancient names so difficult to pronounce, or by long lists of genealogies that are impossible to remember. However, for the earnest believer who aspires to salvation, the permanent study of the Scripture is not an option; it is an unavoidable necessity!

Depending on whether you are interested in the story of God's chosen people, heroic biblical characters, the beautiful stories it contains, or merely seeking to discover and understand the divine messages hidden in the text, the question remains unchanged: how to enter the Bible?

One does not enter the Bible accidentally or inadvertently. The Bible is like a vast mansion with a thousand doors always open to welcome those who wish to come in.

The Iceman Cometh

It was in the early 90' that something twigged me, with the discovery of a natural mummy dating to approximately 5300 years, preserved in ice. Five thousand three hundred years ago, did I say to myself, was the time when the oldest biblical patriarchs lived. The iceman was contemporary with Noah, and he probably lived 15 centuries before Abraham.

The ice man's frozen body was discovered in a glacier in the Tyrolean Alps, on the border between Austria and Italy. Never had the remains of a human so ancient and so well preserved been discovered in the world. The man wore skillfully crafted clothing and high-laced shoes with straw-padded soles, which allowed him to walk in the mountains and glaciers. He had with him a whole panoply of personal items, weapons, and tools, including a magnificent copper ax of superior craftsmanship, and other objects that showed that he must have been a man of high rank. Another sign of his status is that he had been buried with all his valuable belongings.

The ice had so well preserved the cells of the iceman's flesh and the suppleness of his skin, unlike Egyptian mummies, for instance, whose flesh was irremediably altered by the mummification processes that were common practice in ancient Egypt. Thus, researchers were able to extract a wealth of information from it.

We know today, this man died at the age of 45 about 5300 years ago, he was 5' 2", and weighed 130 pounds; we know he had brown hair and brown eyes, and we know that an arrow he received in the shoulder put an end to his life on a beautiful spring day.

In short, this man was probably a genuinely nice man who truly enjoyed life, with whom I would have liked to socialize and have an exciting conversation while sharing a good beer. I would have shown him my smartphone and my new car, and he would assuredly have shown me his unique handmade copper ax, his longbow, and his daunting arrows. But, when I read the reports published by the forensic scientists who studied his remains, it appeared to me that the men who lived over 5000 years ago were not physically different from us who roam on the surface of planet earth today. They had no computers, mobile phones, or other electronic gadgets, but they knew how to survive in a hostile environment, they respected and honored their dead as the good believers they probably were.

What interested me the most, however, was whether, besides the physical aspect of the ancient men of patriarchs' times, their mind and their intellect were sophisticated enough to hold complex reasoning about moral issues, as, for instance, the existence of God. The answer to this question was within my reach. Although the Iceman did not leave written testimonies, the Bible patriarchs who lived in the same period gave us a bountiful number of statements, in writing. Comments about their lives, their struggles, and sufferings, but above all, testimonies of their continuous quest for God and the divine will, their faith, their spirituality, and their great wisdom. I opened my Bible that I had neglected for so long, and with God as my only witness, I started the incredible journey, which, today, I invite you to take in your turn.

Generations of learned and pious men before us have delved into the Scriptures. Thousands of wise men have dedicated their lives to interpreting the signs and complexities of the Word, leaving no stone unturned. The Bible supported God's chosen people through millennia, and we inherited it today to guide and support us and to pass it on to future generations. While it is probably not your intention to immerse yourself deeply into an esoteric study of the Scripture, the wisdom it embodies will enrich your life in countless ways.

The Scripture ought to be read and studied with an open mind.

You will find information new to you, and that could disturb you or upset your preconceptions. Don't be reluctant to pursue your goal, and you will learn how to keep an open mind; and if you accept this information that may be new to you, you will gain a lot in spirituality. Remember that everyone can have their own opinion and there are as many opinions as there are people on earth. You will develop your personal view, but it would be prudent to wait until you are well acquainted with the Scripture.

On the Road Again

At the end of the spiritual adventure you will undertake, God's Spirit will fill you, and you will finally understand the meaning and the purpose that God has assigned to your life. You will get nearer to God, and you'll be able to establish a close personal relationship with him. You'll discover or rediscover how the Scripture that has guided generations of men to recognize the divine presence and the Spirit he put in everyone can today help you.

Remember, it's a journey, not a race. You will travel on an ancient road marked by many generations of men inspired by God. You will enter higher levels of spirituality, especially the seven Bible Laws of Supplication, and your life will never be the same.

Prayer vs. Supplication

"Supplication" (with a capital S) should not be mistaken for "prayer." The two words should not be used interchangeably. There are different prayers, the simple private or common daily prayer; mental or vocal; read, sung, or recited; ardent and fervent or humble; the prayer of thanksgiving or praise; the request, which is also called the prayer of supplication, petition; etc.

Ignore them and bear the consequences

The prayer is conveyed by words that the praying person pronounces aloud or tacitly, while a Supplication is made of commitment and zeal and doesn't need wording.

Supplication and prayer have in common the desire to obtain help and grace from God. Supplication, which is the object of this study, is much more than a prayer, but it is complementary to the prayers of every day. An accomplished Supplication makes all subsequent prayers more meaningful and more effective since the praying person is already nearer to God and recognized by Him.

A Supplication is an act of worship; it is a permanent personal commitment to consecrating oneself to the quest for God and understanding the meaning of the divine will; it is to raise one's soul toward God to express how much they love Him and the exclusive and total adoration one has for Him. The urge to go to God and meet Him justifies a Supplication, knowing that the shortest way to reach God is to love Him.

The careful reading and study of the Bible and your obedience to the Scripture will give you an insatiable thirst for God. Knowledge of the Word will provide you with the strength and the will to engage in the quest for the divine will. But through the practice of Supplication, you will raise your soul toward God.

A Supplication is an act of love and devotion resulting from the union of your will with the divine grace. This short way leads to God and to being admitted into the privileged circle of His chosen ones.

I hope this reading of the Bible's 7 Great Laws will inspire you to read and study the Scriptures more often and to re-read this guide often. I will always remain by your side in your Supplications.

I will pray for you, and pray with you. I invite you to pray also for those who like you, have the will to meet God, so they may succeed, helped by God. Amen!

Ignore them and bear the consequences

Law #1
The Law of Invocation

"Then shall ye call upon me, and ye shall go and pray unto me, and I will hearken unto you." (Jer 29:12)

Your First Supplication

Let's evoke the few minutes that followed your birth. It should not be difficult, as we all went through the same experience. The first thing you probably did was to suck in a deep breath of fresh air and scream to signal to the world you had arrived among us and that your urgent needs had to be satisfied without delay. Emotional and cognitive connections to your mother, your relatives, and to the people living in your household came at a later time; hence, you directed your scream to neither your mother nor anyone else. You sent your shriek to God's providential care, and it was only your first Supplication, probably your most effective one. It was a spontaneous and intuitive deed, rich in teachings. Your parents remember clearly this agitated and noisy event. They recall their baby's face turning red and shaking with convulsions. They recall being seized with panic before they understood how they could; hence satisfy your needs by feeding you and calm you down with necessary cares.

Newborns cannot speak a human language. They are still nearer to God than to man. They ignore the identity of the people surrounding them and their relationship with them. They cannot identify their mother yet. So, they yell at Providence the loudest they can, making sure that their noisy vociferations will convey the sense of emergency as efficiently as ambulances and fire engines can do when a fire occurs in a city. Newborns invoke no one. They ask, and they know that someone will hear their request. The divine Providence always answers the newborn's Supplications. How could it be simpler and more efficient?

Newborns have absolute confidence in the Divine Providence and in those who take care of them, even if they cannot distinguish them. If a mother pretends she will let her baby fall to the ground, their face will not express the slightest fear, and they would not make the slightest attempt to restrain themselves. The confidence of a newborn in the divine providence is absolute, and absolute certainty means faith. Faith in who provides all your needs is the top condition of Supplications. This law is immutable. Ignore it, and you'll irremediably go astray. However, faith does not forbid doubt, although, in Supplication, you must only express faith. Supplication is not the right moment to show your doubts. It is, on the contrary, the ideal moment to sublimate your faith.

Newborns continuously ask, and they ask absolutely everything necessary for them to live and to thrive. However, they only ask for what they need at the very moment when they ask for it, and nothing more. They don't ask for anything extra because their demands are motivated by no other reason than to ensure their survival. At birth, babies know that they fulfill some of the wills of God and that they must do their part in making sure they survive.

Ask with insistence and persistence, and show the highest enthusiasm possible. During your

supplication, you must be convinced that God heard and answered you and that you have received everything you asked in your petition.

Newborns express their needs through unbearable screams, bodily agitation, muscle contractions, and alarming facial expressions. They yell with all the power of their lungs so everyone around can hear it. In these moments, they look like a fire engine responding to an emergency call. They do not choose who must meet their needs among the people who can hear them. Similarly, when you make a petition, it is futile to determine, in the heavenly population, to whom you want to entrust this task. Who are you to interfere in godly affairs?

Newborns instinctively know how to thank those who fulfill their needs. They express their love and gratitude through facial expressions and body language, a smile, for instance, and in many other different ways. Their mothers will soon accustom themselves to their tongues, hence forging a bond of unfailing love that will link mother and child forever.

Newborns, however, do not need to sanctify themselves, because they were born free of any blemishes and are therefore still immaculate. When their acquired knowledge progressively replaces their innate wisdom, they will learn about misconduct and faulty behaviors. When a baby grabs from others something they want for themselves, they learn envy and greed and get accustomed to desiring things that are not essential to their survival. They learn, quite unfairly, to grab others' property. When they are mature enough to be weaned from breastfeeding, they have already developed many bad habits, and that puts a term to the period of grace and innocence that they enjoyed during the first weeks or months of their life. They are pushed out of the Garden of Eden, slowly but surely.

Returning to this state of purity and elevating your soul

Ignore them and bear the consequences

to God will require much effort from the grown-up you have become, but it is an essential and unavoidable requirement for a successful Supplication, as we shall see in law #3, Sanctification. You must learn all over again the things you instinctively knew in the first weeks or months of your life but that you have now forgotten. It is the purpose of this essay to guide you through the whole process.

Scientists know that at birth, you were as good at learning as you will ever be (Lewis P. Lipsitt, Ph.D., Learning Capacities of the Human Infant). Newborns are naturally talented at learning new languages, any language, without exception. Barely a few weeks old, they can discern the subtle contrasts between the specific sounds of any certainty, both in their mother tongue and in any other language, even in tongues to which neither they nor their relatives were ever exposed. Newborns can learn any human language provided they learn it during their prime infancy. Gradually, this extraordinary ability to distinguish sounds diminishes before they even speak, before their first birthday. After the early years, they can no longer discern resonances specific to foreign languages. It is also true for their mother tongue if they have not yet learned the language spoken by their mother.

Scientists believe that losing the newborn's exceptional learning abilities is due to a phenomenon called apoptosis, a natural process of programmed self-destruction of surplus or unused cells aimed at ridding the brain of unemployed neurons. Why not emulate newborns? Would you say? Don't even think about it! Imagine how your friends would react if you yelled and gestured to get what you want. However, let newborns' behavior inspire you. The baby that you once were would have a lot to teach the adult you are today. You can be inspired by the Supplications of your early childhood when your screams, your contorted face, and your alarming newborn convulsions compelled your mother to fulfill your demands right away.

Always ask with insistence and persistence, and show the highest enthusiasm possible. During your supplication, you must be convinced that God heard and answered you and that you have received everything you asked in your petition. The best way to confirm that you are confident that God heard you and answered you is by sending thanksgiving and praises to the Lord for having responded to your pleas and provided for your needs.

However, the newborn is still holy for several weeks following birth, but you're not. To get a result, you will first have to return to your state of purity at birth. Although you should not reasonably expect to reach it 100 percent, consider you succeeded if you just made your best efforts to achieve that goal.

You must get rid of the sins that sully your soul like barnacles on the hull of an old boat returning from a long journey through the oceans of the world. You must do everything you can to sanctify yourself. We'll talk about this more in-depth in Law #3, Sanctification.

Be inspired by the pleas of your early childhood, when you were still holy, and your screams, your contorted face, and your alarming gestures compelled your parents to satisfy your needs without delay. Show in your supplications absolute confidence that God has answered you, even if you have not achieved your Supplication yet. Believe, however, that although you are not yet in possession of what you asked for, you nevertheless own it, because God has vested it upon you. Last but not least, praise the Lord, who provides for all your needs, and be persistent.

Newborns continuously ask, and they ask absolutely everything necessary for them to live and to thrive. However, they only ask for what they need at the very moment when they ask for it, and

Ignore them and bear the consequences

nothing more. They don't ask for anything extra because their demands are motivated by no other reason than to ensure their survival.

To Whom Must Supplications Be Made?

This question is critical. However, the Scriptures could not be more unambiguous, God said "Invoke me, pray to me, and I will hear you." (Cf. Jer 29:12 above.) God revealed what the essence of a Supplication is, and it holds in two short expressions, "invoke me!" and "pray to me!". What seems obvious to many is not always to all, for spiritual leaders, often, look to abide by the famous adage, "Why make things simple when you could make them complicated?" If you set aside the sometimes-complex dogmas, the biblical messages are simple and can easily be understood by everyone, regardless of their level of education or spirituality. If in doubt, look into the Bible. Only the Scripture can be a trusted guide for you. Everything else is but chatter.

You must send your Supplications to God and Him only. Supplications are the highest acts of faith and worship and highly personal and intimate. They strengthen the relationship between a man and his creator. You must not worship any deities other than God. Therefore, it's to God only that you must address your Supplications. "You won't have other gods before me." (Ex 20:3–4; Dt 5:7–8) The Scripture is explicit on this point: you will not worship any deities other than God!

Is God not inaccessible? Quite the contrary! The Bible confirms that it is highly recommended to supplicate to God personally. Christ himself taught his disciples how to say a prayer to God. "After this manner therefore pray ye: Our Father which art in heaven, hallowed be thy name. Thy kingdom come, Thy will be done in earth, as it is in heaven" (Mt 6:9–10).

The Scriptures are full of confirmations about this critical issue. "The Lord hath heard my supplication; the Lord will receive my prayer" (Ps 6:9).

"Hear, O Lord, when I cry with my voice: have mercy also upon me and answer me" (Ps 27:7) "He shall pray unto God, and God will be favorable unto him" (Jb 33:26).

The LORD said, "Then shall ye call upon me, and ye shall go and pray unto me, and I will hearken unto you." (Jer 29:12) When someone tries to seek Him and go to Him, the LORD goes to meet him and takes him by the hand. The Bible says: "And the Lord shall guide thee continually, and satisfy thy soul in drought, and make fat thy bones: and thou shalt be like a watered garden, and like a spring of water, whose waters fail not." (Is 58:11).

The search for the divine becomes easy when the best guide is at your side. "And ye shall seek me, and find me, when ye shall search for me with all your heart. And I will be found of you [I will let myself be found by you]" (Jer 29:13–14).

The Scriptures suggest two other reasons for worshiping and invoking God; each is necessary and sufficient: the forgiveness which He grants and the love which He generously bestows on those who invoke Him. "For thou, Lord, art good, and ready to forgive; and plenteous in mercy unto all them that call upon thee." (Ps 86:5).

The Lord is closer to you than you might think, for God whom you invoke is in you, and you are in him, said Augustine of Hippo.

The Bible says: "If I ascend into heaven, thou art there: if I make my bed in hell, behold, thou art there." (Ps 139:8).

"What? know ye not that your body is the temple of the Holy Ghost which is in you, which ye have of God, and ye are not your own?" (1 Cor 6:19) "But ye are not in the flesh, but in the Spirit, if so be that the Spirit of God dwell in you." (Rom 8:9)

Calling upon the name of God requires that you elevate your

soul toward Him, and solely toward Him.

> **Send your Supplications to God only. Supplications are the highest acts of faith and worship and highly personal. They strengthen the relationship between a man and his creator.**

Idolaters, Ventriloquists and False Prophets

Not invoking God exclusively amounts to practicing idolatry. Idolatry consists in attributing, to man-made objects, powers that God alone possesses. For example, believing in the power of good luck charms that they will bestow good fortune on you or will ward off evil is idolatry, pure and simple.

An idol can have many forms: It may be the image of a saint, a star, a statue, an angel, relics of saints, a fetish, or, any other object which usurps the godly privileges, trespass the celestial domain, and that comes between a believer and God. Idol worship can also be a behavior, an erroneous mental concept, a mental affliction, or even a perversion.

Primitive idol worship is practiced by animists, pagans, and polytheists, who see in their idols, made of inert matter the representation of deities, and believe they have supernatural powers. Once, worshippers made sacrifices and offerings on the altar of such gods, the Scripture says. "Saying to a stock, Thou art my father; and to a stone, Thou hast brought me forth: for they have turned their back unto me, and not their face: but in the time of their trouble they will say, Arise, and save us." (Jer 2:27)

And the Lord says, "But where are thy gods that thou hast made thee? let them arise, if they can save thee in the time of thy trouble" (Jer 2:28)

The idolater trusts another protector, a god created with his own hands. If you think you can serve two masters, one legitimate and one occult, and if between the two your heart swings, you must choose. If you are seeking to find a way to obtain from the occult one those things you asked to the legitimate one, but he refuses to grant you, know that it is impossible.

The Bible says, "No man can serve two masters: for either he will hate the one, and love the other; or else he will hold to the one, and despise the other. Ye cannot serve God and mammon." (Mt 6:24)

Idols need not be recognized and loved; they are not gods and serve only to divert believers from their true God.

To them, the Lord said, "There is none like me in all the earth." (Ex 9:14)

While also pretending to worship God, the idolater maintains an active trade with all kinds of false divinities. The Lord said, "With their lips [they] do honour me, but [they] have removed their heart far from me, and their fear toward me is taught by the precept of men." (Is 29:13) Idols and superstitions are the work of men's hand, and the Scripture says, "They be no gods, which are made with hands" (Acts 19:26)

Primitive idolatry is also alive and flourishing in certain monotheistic religions. Certain denominations which, however, claim to be Christian use pious images, statues of saints or angels, relics taken from the corpses of their saints, or various objects that belonged to these saints; pious medals, lucky fetishes, plus practices such as Marian worship, the worship of saints and angels, all things that meet, clearly and unambiguously, the definition of idolatry.

The primitive forms of idolization are easily identifiable, but a kind of idol worship is more insidious and difficult to fight for it advances with a mask. You are confident that you can hold idolatry at bay, but when hidden behind a mask, will you recognize it? Superstition, to name it. Superstition consists in believing in the supernatural powers of man-made objects or rituals. It is idol worship, period. Delusion is present in your life if you do not do some cleaning as often as needed. The superstitious rely on occult rituals, nothing but idolatrous acts of worship. They hope, thus, to obtain a grace that God does not want to grant them. We will see in Law # 4, Ends & Means, that God disapproves of specific requests found in supplications.

He who practices superstition believes that his idols have quasi-divine powers that will enable him to circumvent divine laws and God's Will, with ease. This form of worship is more offensive to God than proclaimed atheism. Worshiping a saint and believing he will intercede with God for your exclusive benefit is idolatry. All forms of magic evoking occult and supernatural forces to obtain a grace that God does not want to grant you is idolatry. To call on diviners or psychics to conjure the dead or the spirits or to know the future is irrational and delusional, for it amounts to usurping and betraying God (see Law # 4, Ends & Means).

The Bible says: "There shall not be found among you any one that maketh his son or his daughter to pass through the fire, or that useth divination, or an observer of times, or an enchanter, or a witch. Or a charmer, or a consulter with familiar spirits, or a wizard, or a necromancer. For all that do these things are an abomination unto the Lord: and because of these abominations the Lord thy God doth drive them out from before thee." (Dt 18:10–12) It is a serious offense against God.

The Lord said, "Regard not them that have familiar spirits, neither seek after wizards, to be defiled by them: I am the Lord your God." (Lv 19:31).

How can anyone believe that a "good luck" charm, a simple

inanimate man-made object, can bring them happiness, prosperity, protection, or any other benefit? How can they believe that a little silver jewel representing an eye can protect them from the evil eye? All this is only idolatrous fetishism.

But there are still more critical issues. There are seemingly innocuous practices, which can have dramatic effects on your relationship with God, but also your sanity. These practices result from the intrusion of superstitious beliefs in the healthy exercise of faith. Christ defined the basis of worship. He said, "God is a Spirit: and they that worship him must worship him in spirit and in truth." (Jn 4:24).

To worship in spirit is to practice your faith with intelligence and discernment. It is assumed that, when praying, the believer must always have their intelligence wide awake, and that they can use their free will in all things. The Scripture says. "But there is a spirit in man: and the inspiration of the Almighty giveth them understanding." (Jb 32: 8). A religious ritual that does not resist the filter of intelligence and reasoning is only a mechanical ritual devoid of spiritual meaning.

Apostle Paul said, "I will pray with the spirit, and I will pray with the understanding also" (1 Cor 14:15). To worship in truth is to resist the tyranny of religious formalisms with binding rituals, nothing but precepts of human tradition.

The Lord said: "Their fear toward me is taught by the precept of men." (Is 29:13, Mt 15: 8).

To worship in spirit and truth, therefore, is to refuse to be like those Isaiah denounced. The Scripture says, "They have not known nor understood: for he hath shut their eyes, that they cannot see; and their hearts, that they cannot understand." (Is 44:18) Or as those of whom Paul said: "For I bear them record that they have a zeal of God, but not according to knowledge." (Rom 10: 2).

Believing that false deities have the same powers as God is pure hocus-pocus. Worship God and only Him and invoke Him in your prayers and supplications, for Supplication is above all an act of adoration and submission, even if it is also intended to get favors from the Almighty. Supplicating is also designed to affirm your allegiance to God; To lay at His feet your total submission; And to acknowledge that you depend on Him for all your needs.

The Bible says, "Hearken thou to the supplication of thy servant" (1 Kgs 8:30).

Praises and thanksgiving are evident suites to Supplications. Therefore, you must send your petitions to God only, so as not to make you unknowingly guilty of worshipping a false deity. The Bible says: "In everything by prayer and supplication with thanksgiving let your requests be made known unto God." (Phil 4: 6) To invoke God is to seek Him. "Draw near to God, and he will draw near to you." (Jas 4: 8) And not to invoke God is to take the risk of praising and worshipping an illegitimate deity. It means treating the Creator with contempt.

The Bible says: "Shall a man make gods unto himself, and they are no gods?" (Jer 16:20) Strange question! Why ask such a question? The Bible talks of man-made gods carved from materials found on earth, but all their senses seem to have been disabled. These gods are blind, deaf, and dumb. They can neither speak nor hear men who send supplications to them.

The Bible says, "Ye shall serve gods, the work of men's hands, wood, and stone, which neither see, nor hear, nor eat, nor smell." (Dt 4:28, 28:36, 28:64) "The idols of the heathen are silver and gold, the work of men's hands. They have mouths, but they speak not; eyes have they, but they see not; They have ears, but they hear not; neither is there any breath in their mouths. They that make them are like unto them: so is every one that trusteth in them." (Ps 135:15–18).

Elijah, the prophet cried out to the people of Israel, and said, "How long halt ye between two opinions? If the Lord be God, follow him: but if Baal, then follow him." (1 Kgs 18:21) Elijah, put the prophets of Baal to the test. The Bible said: "They called on the name of Baal from morning even until noon, saying, O Baal, hear us. But there was no voice, nor any that answered." (1 Kgs 18:26) Elijah laughed at them, and said to them, "Cry aloud: for he is a god; either he is talking, or he is pursuing, or he is in a journey, or peradventure he sleepeth, and must be awaked." (1 Kgs 18:27) In this passage, I cannot imagine that God did not hear these unfortunate prophets of Baal exhaust themselves to howl in the void, but it is easy to understand why he turned a deaf ear: the prophets of Baal had been invoking an illegitimate divinity.

Idolaters are unaware that the wooden gods are deaf, blind, and dumb. But, would you say, it is ancient history, and Baal no longer exists nowadays? Big mistake! If the name of Baal has disappeared from the scene, Baal is still present among us, but he carries other names and appears in different disguises.

Are you not yet convinced? Let's face it! The seniors among you will remember Charlie McCarthy, the dummy made famous by the great ventriloquist Edgar Bergen, father of actress Candice Bergen. Bergen was so talented that some in his audience sincerely believed that his wooden dummy had the gift of speech. Bergen was an excellent comedian, and his intention was merely to amuse his audience.

If you need further arguments to be convinced, the Scriptures reveal that the power to hear supplicants and to fulfill their requests belongs only to God. The Bible says: "Whatever we ask, we receive it from Him" (1 Jn 3:22) And James confirms: "Every good gift and every perfect gift is from above, and cometh down from the Father of lights" (Jas 1:17) "He shall pray unto God, and he will be favourable unto him" (Jb 33:26) If you need additional evidence, the Bible says: "The Lord hears the prayer of the righteous." (Prv 15:29).

Those who feel God leaves them behind are those who repeatedly make wrong choices, and they have a knack for making bad decisions. They turned away from opportunities that would have allowed them to reconnect with God. Feeling unable to find by themselves a way out of the swamp in which they have become stuck, they then rely on the rhetoric of false prophets, magicians, impostors, and sirens' songs of all kinds. They are marked as easy prey by these charlatans who, like scavengers from far away, can spot carrion.

These skilled talkers do not look as repulsive as scavengers. They even seem kind and generous. Besides, their initial intents are not always evil-driven. The lack of modesty, the need to exercise their power over the weak, but also greed, or, more simply, ignorance is what turns a person into a false prophet.

Ventriloquists are, alas, everywhere. The real ventriloquists are comedians who entertain their audience. However, the ventriloquists referred to herein do not use dummies, and their business is not one of public entertainment. Instead, they are skilled at pretending they speak in the name of God. You may easily spot them because they often use expressions like "God said…" or "God wants…" but their words are nowhere to be found in the Scriptures. They speak like wooden dummies and say words that are not God's words but ventriloquist's empty words. With the Internet and social networks, their chatter is also spreading in writing. It takes a trained mind to spot them, as the Scriptures will never confirm their chatter.

There is another broad category of false prophets. They usurp divine privileges. You have all met people who pretend they can reveal to you where you will be residing after your life on Earth is over. We hear, for example, "Catholics (or any other denomination or faith) will go to hell." Or, "sinners will not go to heaven." That may be true, but how do they know? They are not prophets, to my knowledge. Some want to frighten you by telling you in great detail what your stay in hell will be like for you, as tour operators promoting their best selling all included eternal sojourns in hell. Never having died, they never went there. As for those who have stayed there, none has ever returned. All these false prophets are usurpers, for all these mysteries and other invisible things, only God knows, and he alone can speak of them. If he doesn't talk about it, it is because he wants that stuff he kept hidden from humans to remain that way. "The things which are seen are temporal, but the things which are not seen are eternal." (2 Cor 4:18).

Are intercessors needed?

God doesn't share His rank and privileges with anyone. "My glory will I not give to another" (Is 42: 8) This verse indicates that God alone is empowered to hear a Supplication and that he does not intend to share this power and privilege with anyone. Divine blessings, gifts, for example, are part of those graces which God has reserved for Himself. We will see in Law # 4, End & Means, that you must not ask those things which God has reserved for Himself the right and privilege to decide alone, with no influence.

Make your Supplications to God, directly, and to no one else. The Scriptures are clear on this point. The Bible says: "They shall call on my name, and I will hear them" (Zec 13: 9) "Call unto me, and I will answer thee" (Jer 33:3) Through your Supplication, you will go to God, and you will have an encounter with Him. The Bible says: "He shall pray unto God, and he [God] will be favourable unto him" (Jb 33:26) Your petitions are useless if they are not sent directly to God. Using the services of an intercessor is unnecessary, and may even be risky. "If we ask anything according to his will, he heareth us" (1 Jn 5:14)

Is it OK to try anyway?

If you address a supplication to a deity other than our Lord, God, it is not only vain, but it may also be an offense against the Lord. The Bible says: "To whom then will ye liken God? or what likeness will ye compare unto him?" (Is 40:18) If you do it knowingly, what you do is as disastrous as worshiping idols, practicing magic, or using a superstitious practice to procure you unduly what you may not ask God.

Intercessors are nothing but idols, and like all idols, they are man-made, according to the Bible. "Their idols are silver and gold, the work of men's hands." (Ps 115:4).

What If I Err in Good Faith?

Those who wander in good faith have nothing to fear. God knows the true intentions of everyone. He will not systematically ignore their requests, for God's designs are superior, and His divine will is sovereign, but those who persist in error without ever amending themselves, are not ready to come close to the Lord and to feel the warmth of His presence. In the best of cases, their supplications are more likely to meet the fate of the thousands of letters lost every day because the name and address of the recipient written on the envelope are wrong.

Intercession of Saints and Angels

Nothing can alter the Divine Will, and no one, neither the saints nor the angels nor the storm nor the beautiful weather, can influence the Lord in His decisions. No one can or ought to overstep the limits of God's private domain, for God's will is sovereign. What do you expect from an intercessor? That he represents you before God, for you think that the involvement of someone highly regarded in the heavenly sphere will help your cause, as you would hire a lawyer to represent you in a court of justice? Some lawyers would not hesitate to make you believe that they know someone best friends with yet another person who is friends with the judge's brother-in-law.

It is true, though, that it is not a bad idea to be represented in court by a lawyer to plead your case, because the law is complex and often confusing for a non-lawyer. Judges do not have the gift of reading what litigants hide in their hearts. But before God, it is useless to plead, for God knows what everyone has in mind. The Bible says: "Thou, even thou only, knowest the hearts of all the children of men." (1 Kgs 8:39) Just make an effort to introduce yourself in person—no matter what language you use to talk to God. You don't need to know any technical or professional jargon to speak to Him. Everyone can communicate with God in their language and with their own simple words, like a child babbling to his father. The child's father understands him perfectly, without having to translate child talks into grown-up language.

God's mercy and generosity are infinitely more significant than that of the holiest among the saints, therefore, your chances of being heard and getting what you ask for are higher when you speak directly to him. By involving himself personally in the well-being of his children and providing for their needs, God fixes injustices and grants success and prosperity to all those making him the request, according to their needs, as would a father with his children, thus ensuring the balance, harmony, and sustainability of his great Creation.

The angels are God's servants, and they serve him exclusively,

Ignore them and bear the consequences

according to the Bible. "Bless the Lord, ye his angels, that excel in strength, that do his commandments." (Ps 103:20)

When Manoah's barren wife learned from God's angel she would bear a son, Manoah invoked the Lord and prayed to him, "O my Lord, let the man of God which thou didst send come again unto us, and teach us what we shall do unto the child that shall be born." (Jgs 13: 8) and God heard his prayer. As God had sent an angel to bring the good news to Manoah's wife, the latter did the right thing, invoking God, not the angel, urging Him to send His messenger again to tell him what to do once the child is born. It is, therefore, vain to turn the angels away from their mission, which is to serve God, to put them in your service.

The fear of appearing before God drives those who think they need an intercessor. They are loaded with sins and prefer to be represented, if, however, this was possible. They believe they could maneuver by seeking the mediation of a third party closer to God as if to bribe him. Mary, the mother of Christ, is often solicited. The most recognized saints are equally so, by the impudent ones who think they can convince them to work as their servants. But the Saints are only humans, and the Bible says, "He [God] putteth no trust in his saints" (Jb 15:15)

God is not inaccessible, quite the contrary, and instead, the Scriptures are unanimous in sanctioning that you can and should call upon him directly.

Invoking Mary, Mother of Christ?

The Scriptures do not say that Jesus or anyone else praised or worshiped Mary. Nowhere, in the Scripture, is it suggested that you can invoke Mary or that Mary can intercede with God. The Scriptures say that Mary is a servant of God, obedient and pious and that she became the mother of Jesus. Mary had received grace from God, the Bible says. "The angel came in unto her, and said, Hail, thou that art highly favoured, the Lord is with thee: blessed art thou among women." (Lk 1:28) This grace was the redemption of her sins. For Mary, as a human, was a sinner, like every other being of flesh. "There is not a just man upon earth, that doeth good, and sinneth not." (Eccl 7:20).

Mary was grateful to God for having been saved. "My soul doth magnify the Lord, And my spirit hath rejoiced in God my Saviour. For he hath regarded the low estate of his handmaiden: for, behold, from henceforth all generations shall call me blessed. For he that is mighty hath done to me great things; and holy is his name." (Lk 1:46–49) The Bible does not say that Mary had the power to intercede with God.

The Scriptures are straightforward: you must worship God exclusively. Those who were in the service of God refused unequivocally to let people invoke them.

Peter and the apostles refused to be worshiped. The Scriptures say: "As Peter was coming in, Cornelius met him, and fell down at his feet, and worshipped him. But Peter took him up, saying, Stand up; I myself also am a man." (Acts 10:25–26).

The angels refuse to be worshiped. "And I fell at his feet to worship him. And he said unto me, See thou do it not: I am thy fellow servant, and of thy brethren that have the testimony of Jesus: worship God: for the testimony of Jesus is the spirit of prophecy." (Rv 19:10) "See thou do it not: for I am thy fellow servant, and of thy brethren the prophets, and of them which keep the sayings of this book: worship God." (Rv 22: 9).

Calling Upon the Name of Christ?

Christ himself taught his disciples how to pray to God: "When ye pray, use not vain repetitions, as the heathen do: for

Ignore them and bear the consequences

they think that they shall be heard for their much speaking. Be not ye therefore like unto them: for your Father knoweth what things ye have need of, before ye ask him." (Mt 6:7–13)

In the days of his flesh, Christ often had recourse to supplications. Supplication was the essence of his relationship with God. He supplicated for himself, for the success of his mission, and his adepts.

To obtain the wisdom he needed to choose his twelve apostles, Jesus invoked the Lord in Supplication, according to the Bible. "He [Jesus] went out into a mountain to pray, and continued all night in prayer to God. And when it was day, he called unto him his disciples: and of them he chose twelve, whom also he named apostles" (Lk 6:12–13)

Shortly before his death on the cross, he addressed pathetic supplications to the Lord for his own salvation.

The Bible says, "He had offered up prayers and supplications with strong crying and tears unto him that was able to save him from death" (Heb 5:7)

Christ addressed supplications to God the Father, asking for protection from temptation. "O my Father, if it be possible, let this cup pass from me: nevertheless not as I will, but as thou wilt." (Mt 26:39)

Jesus also supplicated for all his followers: "I pray for them: I pray not for the world, but for them which thou hast given me; for they are thine." (Jn 17:9) On the cross, he prayed to beg the Lord to forgive those who committed blasphemy against him. "Father, forgive them; for they know not what they do." (Lk 23:34)

Can We Call Upon the Holy Spirit?

You must call upon God, for the Holy Spirit intercedes by himself if that is His desire, without you having to call on Him.

When you invoke God, there can be no ambiguity.

The Bible says "The Spirit itself maketh intercession for us with groanings which cannot be uttered." (Rom 8:26). If you are in doubt, refer to the Scriptures. The apostle said, "Abraham believed God, and it was counted unto him for righteousness." (Rom 4:3).

"All scripture is given by inspiration of God, and is profitable for doctrine, for reproof, for correction, for instruction in righteousness." (2 Tm 3:16)

> **You must invoke the Lord your God exclusively. To be heard, your Supplication requests that you call upon the name of God. Invoking God is necessary and sufficient, according to the Scripture. "Whosoever shall call upon the name of the Lord shall be saved." (Jl 2:32, Rom 10:13, Acts 2:21)**

Calling Upon a Beloved Departed

Your departed loved one is still alive in you, although he left behind him his carnal body and with it all material concerns, emotions, feelings, and passions. All the love he had for you, he deposited it deep into your heart, where it remains for as long as you keep his memory alive. You must let the departed ascend to God, and do not hinder their ascent by trying to bring them back to you. It is their licit privilege. Death is deliverance. It is the privilege of the departed to be relieved of earthly duties so that their soul may merge into the Spirit. When you need them, draw from the legacy they left in your heart. Everything is there. But do not mistakenly invoke them in your supplications. You must only invoke God. The dead can no longer hear you. The voice you might listen to could be the echo of your inner voice

Ignore them and bear the consequences

crying out your distress or that of evil demons who would try to deceive you by taking advantage of your disarray.

As explained in Law # 4, Ends & Means, there are things God does not want to reveal to His children: the future, the afterlife, prenatal memories, the date of their death, or anyone else's death, for instance. These things are part of the areas that God keeps for Himself. It is useless to understand why; simply respect His will. That is why those who claim to read the future or communicate with the dead are only greedy and mischievous tricksters who want to make their victims believe that they have quasi-divine powers and can bypass God's will.

The diviners, psychics, soothsayers, necromancers, and fortune tellers, are merely impostors, and God hates them. The mere fact of calling upon their services or attempting to violate the private domain which God has reserved for Himself is a grave sin, an offense to God. You should neither meddle in the abode of the dead nor interfere with those who are no longer alive. Christ said, "Let the dead bury their dead" (Mt 8:22, and Lk 9:60) so the dead are in another world, the kingdom of God, and that it is useless to solicit them.

God does not want you to socialize with the dead or the demons. For, by calling upon the deceased, you may create a fellowship with a devil. To emulate a psychic is nothing but black magic, witchcraft, and idol worship. The Scriptures are clear on this point.

The Bible says, "I would not that ye should have fellowship with devils. Ye cannot drink the cup of the Lord, and the cup of devils: ye cannot be partakers of the Lord's table, and of the table of devils" (1 Cor 10:20–21)

Death is deliverance. It is the privilege of the departed to be relieved so they may merge into

the Spirit. When you need them, draw from the endowment they left deep in your heart. Everything is there. But do not mistakenly invoke them in your supplications. You must only invoke God.

What did Augustine Think?

According to Augustine of Hippo, the dead, including the saints, live another life in another dimension. Nothing connects them with the world of the earthlings. The departed do not interfere with the lives of the living, because they do not know what the livings think, do, feel, and why they pray.

By entering into their new heavenly life, they left behind their feelings, their desires, their hopes, for they now possess everything and have no longer any need, longing or wish. It is therefore vain to implore their aid and to call upon them, for they cannot help you.

What did Thomas Aquinas Think?

Thomas Aquinas said: "Jesus himself, as a man, is called the Holy of Holies, and as such, he must pray. However, we never ask Christ to pray for us. Therefore, we should not ask the other saints to intercede in our name with God."

Why do we have to Ask God?

Since God knows everything, why do we have to ask him what we need? It is not conceivable that you sit idly and hope to be heard from heaven, because Supplications are much more than a simple phone call or text message sent from your smartphone to the celestial sphere. A Supplication is, above all, an act of

Ignore them and bear the consequences

faith and a highly personal and intimate act of worship from men toward their creator. The supplication implies, on your part, the existence of a strong desire and a personal commitment to elevating yourself to God and be allowed for a moment to have an encounter with him.

God sometimes bestows gifts you never thought of soliciting, and he does so often, but He asks to be recognized and revered. It is not vanity, but just as a father plays with his children, but always ensures that his children do not act toward him like with their friends of the same age.

A self-respecting father asks that his children respect him and acknowledge his authority, even if he rarely exercises it. On these conditions, he accepts to play freely with them and creates a link of trust, love, and respect.

If you are not always turned to God, how can you hope to be heard without going to Him? If you are not sure that God will hear you, how can you hope to receive?

The Bible says, "He regarded their affliction, when he heard their cry." (Ps 106: 44).

Supplication is a long solitary journey. All great travelers know that if arriving at a destination brings great satisfaction, the voyage is a much more rewarding experience.

If by the end of your life, you have never completed a supplication, that would mean you did not live and never cared about your spirituality and relationship with God. Your soul will end up with others in the landfill of creation.

What Does the Scripture Say?

The Scriptures reveal that God has limited trust in angels and saints. They are His faithful and blessed servants, they are close to him, but they are not of the divine essence; They are human, and as such, they are fallible and prone to making mistakes.

The Scripture says, "Behold, he [God] put no trust in his servants; and his angels he charged with folly." (Jb 4:18).

God considers them to be imperfect. He blames them for their vanities and their weaknesses. He says that they are no better than the living, even if their life in the flesh was exemplary, and they are higher than the mass of humans.

How can we think for a moment that God could have entrusted them with the mission of interceding on behalf of those who live on earth? The Scripture says, "He [God] putteth no trust in his saints" (Jb 15:15).

God wants you to call upon His name personally, directly, and exclusively. He does not need help from anyone to communicate with His children. It is unnecessary to call upon intercessors to speak to him because he alone knows what His children need. The Bible says, "Whatsoever we ask, we receive of him" (1 Jn 3:22).

Fallen in disgrace by the Will of God, Job rebels against the injustice of which he thinks he is a victim, and he argues in front of his friends, the wise Eliphaz of Teman, Bildad of Shuah, and Zophar of Naama, who comforted him.

Eliphaz's reply is unambiguous: if God does not hear your supplications, what saint will do? The Scripture says, "Call now, if there be any that will answer thee; and to which of the saints wilt thou turn?" (Jb 5:1). This verse suggests that none of the saints would answer, for no one, neither saints nor angels can act as a substitute for God.

During this same conversation, Eliphaz's counsel is clear: call upon the name of God! "I would seek unto God, and unto

Ignore them and bear the consequences

God would I commit my cause"

When Jeremiah wrote to the people of Jerusalem deported to Babylon by Nebuchadnezzar, a few months earlier, in the year 597 BC, he explained to them they should not hope to return to Jerusalem before the 70 years of their exile have expired, and he tried to persuade them to settle in Babylon as if they stayed there forever. In his letter, he reminds them of the promise of the Lord "Then shall ye call upon me, and ye shall go and pray unto me, and I will hearken unto you." (Jer 29:12).

In hearing the specific supplications of those who call upon him, God does not solely satisfy the selfish needs of these men. When the Lord hears someone and fulfills his petition, His graces also benefit, directly or indirectly, many lives. When he sends the rain from the sky, rivers swell, fields are watered, and his gift supports the growth of myriads of living beings, plants, insects, birds, livestock, vegetables and fruit crops, to finally benefit villages and towns inhabited by thousands of men, in compliance with God's own divine will. As we'll see in #2, God has assigned to each one of his creatures the duty of acting as a conduit for dispensing his gifts through a complex network that requires the collective participation of all beings who depend on it. As in a philharmonic orchestra, should a single player depart from the score, and the whole performance would be irreparably damaged. In the realm of life, plants and animals are respectful of God's will. As for the human species, it is otherwise, by their lack of will, discipline, and respect for the divine creation. By obstructing the proper functioning of the God willed network you become guilty of committing a severe transgression to the holy Will.

Whom did David turn to, when, in the depth of despair, he felt an imminent life-threatening danger approaching? "Hear, O Lord, when I cry with my voice: have mercy also upon me, and answer me." David knows, humbly and sincerely, that God hears him. He is confident, for he knows that God hears those who call upon him. Raising his hands towards heaven, where the divine sanctuary is found, in the traditional gesture that accompanied prayer. It is to God himself that he addresses his supplication "Hear the voice of my supplications, when I cry unto thee, when I lift up my hands toward thy holy oracle." (Ps 28:2). David has absolutely no doubt that God will help him. "As for me, I will call upon God; and the Lord shall save me." (Ps 55:16)

When the psalmist feels like he is stuck deep in an abyss from which no one can save him, he turns to God again, "Out of the depths have I cried unto thee, O Lord. Lord, hear my voice: let thine ears be attentive to the voice of my supplications." (Ps 130:1–2); And, "In the day of my trouble I will call upon thee: for thou wilt answer me." (Ps 86:7); And, "I said unto the Lord, Thou art my God: hear the voice of my supplications, O Lord." (Ps 140: 6); And again: "Hear my prayer, O Lord, give ear to my supplications: in thy faithfulness answer me, and in thy righteousness." (Ps 143: 1).

God gives like fathers give to their children, but God gives better than a father, for He knows better than a father what his children need. "If ye then, being evil, know how to give good gifts unto your children, how much more shall your Father which is in heaven give good things to them that ask him?" (Mt 7:11)

As explained in Law #3, Sanctification, invoking God is the most appropriate way to regain a state of sanctity, particularly suitable to those seeking intimacy with God. To become intimate with God, you must clean a great deal. Why do you put on your best-looking attire to go to church on Sunday, if you think it is fine to appear before God with a soul heavy with sins? The Lord said to Abraham, "Walk before me, and be thou perfect." (Gn 17:1)

In hearing the specific supplications of those who call upon him, God does not solely satisfy the selfish needs of these men.

Ignore them and bear the consequences

When the Lord hears someone and fulfills his petition, His graces also benefit, directly or indirectly, many lives. When He sends the rain from the sky, rivers swell, fields are watered, and support the growth of myriads of living beings, plants, insects, birds, livestock, vegetables, and fruit crops, to finally benefit villages and towns inhabited by thousands of humans, in compliance with God's own Divine will.

Law #2
The Law of God's Will

"Ask now the beasts, and they shall teach thee; and the fowls of the air, and they shall tell thee: Or speak to the earth, and it shall teach thee: and the fishes of the sea shall declare unto thee." (Jb 12:7–8)

Understanding the Will of God

You passionately aspire to understand what God's Will means, for you want to live a life that is in harmony with His Will. The Bible says, "Teach me to do thy will; for thou art my God." (Ps 143:10) But even if you are assiduous in the quest for divine will, you must acknowledge your frequent failures, your mistakes, your frustrations, and your difficulties in fully understanding what Divine Will means. In fact, it is not always easy to understand what God expects of us, for His ways are different, and so much more complicated than ours. The Scripture says, "My thoughts are not your thoughts, neither are your ways my ways, saith the Lord." (Is 55: 8).

You then resign yourself to thinking that to see God's plans is simply out of reach, too complicated, or that His will is also challenging to interpret, and you infer that you have no other recourse but to rely on those, you suppose, are capable of understanding what you do not understand. Here also, you meet with disappointment.

You want to understand, but you feel a bit lost when facing the immensity of the task. Your questions remain unanswered. What seemed important to you isn't anymore, and what you had taken for granted, you must now question it. You are not alone in this situation, even the most knowledgeable people discover with surprise that what they thought to be God's Will was only the reflection of their own will, altered by that of third parties and mixed with abstruse clichés, all produced by human minds, which, though commendable, are erroneous, for they do not reflect the Word of God. The Bible says, "Be ye not unwise, but understanding what the will of the Lord is." (Eph 5:17).

Understanding the Divine Will is the first step toward spiritual fulfillment and the indispensable prerequisite for any Supplication. To seek what is the Holy Will is to search for God himself. The Bible says, "ye shall seek me, and find me, when ye shall search for me with all your heart. And I will be found of you, saith the Lord" (Jer 29:13–14)

Divine Providence never leaves anything to chance. If the quest for God's will appears to be difficult, it is by design. The clergy, the religious authority, are neither prophets nor messengers of God. The Bible says, "In vain they do worship me, teaching for doctrines the commandments of men." (Mt 15:9) The most respected spiritual guides sometimes lose themselves in subtleties far too learned to conform to what God wants. They certainly help with their excellent advice, but you must remain vigilant not to substitute their words for the Word of God.

You should neither be swayed by humans nor by the precepts they created; by dogmas nor by false prophets. Don't let anyone come between you and God, in your quest of His will.

The divine message is always proclaimed in plain language accessible to all. God knows how to make himself understood with simple words. His word does not need to be supported by evidence and is not susceptible to being contradicted. If an interpretation of the divine word seems too complicated for you, it is because something was lost in translation. God doesn't only talk to scholars and theologians. He speaks to each of his children. The Bible is full of these simple messages and easy-to-interpret metaphors. Albert Einstein used to say, "If you cannot explain it to a six-year-old, it's because you did not understand it." This saying is particularly true when applied to the study of the divine will.

God's will is not a mystery that insiders alone can understand. It can be understood by anyone who is willing to make the necessary effort to understand it. Before going any further, ask yourself these preliminary questions: do you really want to understand what the divine will is? Are you willing to accept what will be revealed to you? Are you resolved to renounce the moral and intellectual comfort in which you are now contented, to question conventional beliefs, and to make room for the truth? More importantly, you must be sure of your intentions, for it is better to remain in the cozy comfort of ignorance than to understand God's will and not work toward its accomplishment.

If your spiritual guide fails to give you a satisfactory answer, take your questions to a higher level. Take the challenge of finding the solution by yourself. Take the commitment to solve this most important question with the tools God gifted you with. God has endowed you with two exceptional tools, mind and intelligence, so why don't you use them? You should know, by now, that God's word is always simple to explain, simple to understand, and easily verifiable. God doesn't want you to let yourself be led by the leash like a mule. The Scripture says: "Be ye not as the horse, or as the mule, which have no understanding." (Ps 32:9) He created man to rule over animals, not be led like cattle; God said, "let them

Ignore them and bear the consequences

[humans] have dominion over the fish of the sea, and over the fowl of the air, and over the cattle, and over all the earth, and over every creeping thing that creepeth upon the earth." (Gn 1:26) If your spiritual guide fails you, God is there to guide you, if you ask him, in all wisdom and with intelligence; The Bible says, "that ye might be filled with the knowledge of his will in all wisdom and spiritual understanding" (Col 1:9) And, "The Lord shall guide thee continually" (Is 58:11) Let yourself be guided by the safest guide. The Scripture says, "Thy word is a lamp unto my feet, and a light unto my path." (Ps 119:105).

God wants you to make personal efforts to understand His will and to undertake this journey toward Him, even if, at first glance, it may seem out of your reach. That is what gives Him the greatest pleasure, and it is his will. This is why scholarly discourses and complex theories of those who act according to the principle "why make it simple when one can make it complicated" are covered with a veil of opacity, even when their authors are the best-intentioned. The Bible says: "Be ye not unwise, but understanding what the will of the Lord is." (Eph 5:17) This verse reveals that you must not be content with ready-made answers or commonly accepted beliefs, but make your best effort to study with an open mind and not be scared by what you understand.

One day, your turn will come to undertake the great journey in quest of God and of his divine will, for as long as you have not attempted to elevate yourself toward him, you will have no personal relationship with Him, and your requests will often remain unanswered. The Bible says: "The Lord is good unto them that wait for him, to the soul that seeketh him." (Lam 3:25)

Some feel the need to focus on the Divine Will only when they are going through personal hardship; they don't know how to solve an issue, or they are reluctant to make an important decision for themselves or a loved one without guidance. Others start to be interested in the subject when they have a severe illness, or when they are getting older, and the prospect of getting closer to the term of their life causes them to do what they should have done long ago. However, the quest for God and the divine will is an initiatory journey that you need to start as early in your life as possible, or as soon as you become conscious of this much important spiritual issue, because the longer you wait, the harder the task will be.

If you seriously want to commit yourself to such a great adventure, the Lord will be with you, and He will guide you throughout the journey, like a father who teaches his son to take his first steps. The Bible says, "I will instruct thee and teach thee in the way which thou shalt go: I will guide thee with mine eye." (Ps 32:8) When you need help, ask Him, like David, who invoked God and asked, "Teach me to do thy will." (Ps 143:10) James teaches that it's up to you to make the first step, and he suggests how to proceed; The Bible says, "Draw nigh to God, and he will draw nigh to you." (Jas 4:8)

Who Can Teach What God's Will Is?

Don't think that it would be simpler to question the religious authority, or to content yourself with what biblical commentators say about it. Although they are honest and willing to help, they are not prophets. Likewise, as you studied in Law # 1, Invocation, don't rely on an intercessor to appear before God in your stead. Do not rely on the intelligence and wisdom of others to understand what the divine will is. Supplications, as well as the quest for God's Will, are intrinsically intertwined in a supreme act of personal and intense worship towards the Lord.

You must understand by yourself what the Divine Will is, through your own will and your own intelligence. The Bible says,

Ignore them and bear the consequences

"The anointing which ye have received of him abideth in you, and ye need not that any man teach you." (1 Jn 2:27) The Anointing that this verse is referring to is the divine Spirit that dwells in you. Rather than seeking confirmation from other men, even learned theologians, ministers, or distinguished commentators, you must validate it by making use of your own will, your own efforts, and your own intelligence.

The quest for God's will is an act of personal and intense worship toward the Lord. The Lord said, "Ye shall seek me, and find me, when ye shall search for me with all your heart. And I will be found of you, saith the Lord" (Jer 29:13–14) You must do, all by yourself, what needs to be done to seek and to understand what the divine will is, through your own will and your own intelligence.

Your Personal Quest for God

Do not confuse God's plan and design for you, that is, the assignment that God has entrusted to you and what he wants you to do, on the one side, and the personal choices you make throughout your life. If what you are looking for is what your future will look like, your professional successes, your wealth, and prosperity, this guide won't bring you the answers you need. However, if you want to understand that God's will is that you conform your life to His will, that you serve Him, and that you get closer to Him, then, you are on the right track. The Scripture says, "If any man will do his will, he shall know of the doctrine, whether it be of God, or whether I speak of myself." (Jn 7:17)

God Is Immutable

Before creation, God's Will already was, for God and God's Will is one, everlasting, unique, almighty, and immutable. God's will is immutable; It never changes. All that God has created bears His imprint. Consequently, you can read in His work as an open book. God's Creation is not immutable, for God could one day decide to put an end to heaven, earth, the universe, and all the living beings He created, but He will remain forever, for He is immutable. The Bible says, "Thou [Lord] art the same, and thy years shall have no end." (Ps 102: 27, Heb 1:12) And the Lord said, "I am the Lord, I change not." (Mal 3:6)

God and His will are immutable, as is His Word; The Bible says, "Forever, O Lord, thy word is settled in heaven." (Ps 119:89) And "The word of the Lord endureth forever." (1 Pt 1:25) And, "Heaven and earth shall pass away, but my words shall not pass away." (Mt 24:35) Divine love is likewise immutable and eternal; the Scripture says, "The Lord hath appeared of old unto me, saying, Yea, I have loved thee with an everlasting love." (Jer 31:3) God's mercy, likewise, knows no end; "The Lord is good; his mercy is everlasting; and his truth endureth to all generations." (Ps 100:5) The salvation promised by the Lord is, therefore, immutable, and this should reassure you, for, if you abide by His will, you may totally rely on the divine promise of redemption of sins and eternal life.

In your quest for God's will, don't let your mind and your free will go down into mental passivity; don't let your spirit and your intelligence become dormant. God is closer to those who look like the souls who dwell in heaven, angels, and saints. The Bible says, "Strong meat belongeth to them that are of full age, even those who by reason of use have their senses exercised to discern both good and evil." (Heb 5:14) The Lord said, "The man is become as one of us, to know good and evil." (Gn 3:22).

Ignore them and bear the consequences

Don't passively conform to commonly accepted opinions and beliefs of your time, to preconceived ideas, even when they have the endorsement of established authorities. These ready-to-use preconceived ideas are to your intelligence what processed foods are to your palate. Instead, use your own brain, your own wisdom, and critical thinking. Always challenge your own judgments. The Bible says, "Be not conformed to this world: but be ye transformed by the renewing of your mind, that ye may prove what is that good, and acceptable, and perfect, will of God." (Rom 12:2).

Should you strongly desire to understand what the Divine Will is, behold the holy work around you and try to find out the reason why God created it that way. This quest involves a three-pronged process: a) The study of God's Word, the Scripture. Amazingly, the Scripture contains the answers to all the questions that everyone asked or will ever ask; b) Observe God created nature around you with an open and critical mind; Look for clues and examples that the Lord has generously disseminated all over his Creation; c) Confirm the result of your findings through your understanding and your intelligence.

The Scripture, Word of God

God reveals himself to us through his Word in which he is totally and eternally present. His Word reveals God as he truly is, holy, merciful, and faithful. God and His Word are one. He does not change and will never change. God's Word is eternal and immutable. God is the guarantor of his Word; that's why you may place your trust in him.

The Bible says, "All scripture is given by inspiration of God, and is profitable for doctrine, for reproof, for correction, for instruction in righteousness." (2 Tm 3:16) The fact that it was revealed by men, the prophets who received it from God and who transcribed it in writing, takes nothing away from its divine origin and its immutable and infallible nature. The prophets who revealed and transcribed it were inspired by the Spirit of God. The Bible says, "The prophecy came not in old time by the will of man: but holy men of God spake as they were moved by the Holy Ghost." (2 Pt 1:21).

It is to this Word that you must refer, in all your acts and all your biblical studies. It must be the sole judge for everything that can influence you. The Bible says, "Thy word is true from the beginning: and every one of thy righteous judgments endureth for ever." (Ps 119:160) And "Thy word is truth." (Jn 17:17)

The Scripture preserved for us God's Word and the testimonies of several generations of predecessors. They left us the precious spiritual heritage of our ancestors in their quest for God and His will. The questions you ask yourself today, generation after generation, wise men have asked the same before you. Their questions, their doubts, their mistakes, their sufferings, their joy of understanding what God wants, have been carefully reported in the Scripture, for us, and all future generations. The Bible says, "Do ye think that the scripture saith in vain?" (Jas 4:5) This is where you need to start. The Word of God is living, and today it speaks to us through the Scripture, for His will is immutable.

One difficulty you will encounter lies in the fact that you will need to make sure that you understand the divine message as it is revealed in the Scripture and not a reworded version that has been reviewed and corrected by well-intentioned commentators or overzealous translators. Don't just learn verses by heart but do use your critical intelligence to verify that your understanding is not fundamentally different from that of the biblical author. If necessary, use different translations of the Bible.

At this stage of your study, you made tremendous progress, so, don't give up on the pretext that it seems too hard, and don't renounce to succeed by yourself, thinking that a spiritual advisor will give you the answers you need in less time and with no efforts. Don't believe that after all, the clergy and the theologians are supposed to understand these things better, and if you ask them, they will explain it to you in a snap. This reasoning is wrong because the level of complexity of biblical text interpretation is proportional to the educational level of those who devote themselves to it. Exegetical commentators may search for complex philosophical questions in a text, for it is the nature of their scholarly specialty, but most people would just seek the meaning that the sacred author intended to convey through his writing. The scholar and the regular guy will ask different questions, and they will deduce different answers, but each will be content with it, for the answers they get will correspond to their reciprocal expectations. Be convinced that God gives the same value to the efforts of a theologian as to those of a student, and as far as biblical studies are concerned, your work is as valuable as that of any scholar.

Why is God's Will Not In Writing?

The answer to this question is simple and self-explanatory. The Lord has filled your heart with wisdom and your mind with intelligence because he wants you to use these beautiful gifts. The commandments, on the other hand, merely require adherence, obedience, and humility, prior to understanding their purpose. In other words, like a loving father, God extends his arms wide open and helps you find your way to Him. However, God wants you to make an effort to seek Him, to see Him, and to go to Him.

Once your determination is affirmed, He will take you by the hand and lead you to Him. The Lord said, "Ye shall seek me, and find me, when ye shall search for me with all your heart. And I will be found of [by] you" (Jer 29:13–14) and "Who hath put wisdom in the inward parts? or who hath given understanding to the heart?" (Jb 38:36).

God gave His commandments to Moses for the Hebrew people. The commandments, of course, are part of his Will, but they are not the sole expression of it. The word "Commandments" is not used in the singular, to indicate the plurality of divine requirements to those who believe in him. This plurality suggests that the list is not exhaustive and that God wants us to understand his commandments in their broadest sense. The word "Will" on the other hand, is always in the singular, for God's Will is one and indivisible, eternal, and immutable. The Divine Will has not been explained in a book or on tablets. God wanted it that way so that each one of his children would have to provide a personal effort of research and to understand what his Will consists of.

Understanding God's Will Through Observation

The empirical study of creation is based on the observation of nature and natural phenomena and, more importantly, of the behavior of living creatures. It is an essential step in the quest for the Divine Will. It consists in exploring how living creatures, animals and plants, and natural elements interact to participate in the accomplishment of the Divine Will. The careful observation of the divine work is indicative of God's Will, which is one and indivisible, and which is exerted evenly on all things and all beings created by God. Thus, observing God's Will in action in the immutable performances of nature through the lens of your

Ignore them and bear the consequences

critical intelligence, you can easily deduce the meaning of his Will. The Bible says: "Ask now the beasts, and they shall teach thee; and the fowls of the air, and they shall tell thee: Or speak to the earth, and it shall teach thee: and the fishes of the sea shall declare unto thee." (Jb 12:7–8).

In the divine work, everything, every living creature, every event, has a God-designed meaning and purpose. You have been, so far, unresponsive to these apparent manifestations of the Divine Will, because your state of alertness was not awake. You never thought by yourself of questioning the beasts and the birds of the sky or of speaking to the earth. But now that you are aware of it, it will be quite different. When you do your daily walk as always, you will realize that you can see many more things than you never noticed before, although nothing has changed in the familiar landscape of your walk.

As part of the divine creation, the earth itself participates in the accomplishment of his will, when, gorged with rainwater, it grows grass that feeds animals and plants that sustain men. The Bible says, "The earth which drinketh in the rain that cometh oft upon it, and bringeth forth herbs meet for them by whom it is dressed, receiveth blessing from God." (Heb 6:7).

Ask the Beasts, the Birds of the Sky

A bee lands on a flower by the roadside. Ask the bee, and it will teach you. Bees fly from flower to flower to collect pollen and gorge themselves with nectar. In so doing, they pollinate the flowers, carrying pollen from the stamen of one flower to the pistil of others. Many plants cannot perform this operation by themselves, though it is essential to reproduction. Bees, therefore, do much more than feed themselves and provide for their hive. They also, incidentally and in a subliminal way, accomplish the Will of God, by ensuring, with their pollination work, the everlasting sustainability of his creation. Bees and wind are the main natural pollination agents. The powerful winds carry pollen and seeds across oceans and sow them over distant lands. Bees are relentless servants of God. They do a crucial job by carrying out the pollination of flowering plants. A simple bee! What a stunning example! What can the observation of the life of this tiny insect teach you about the Will of God?

It's simple to understand. There is no need for reading scholarly studies or seeking advice from a wise man. God wants each of his creatures to participate in the flawless functioning and the sustainability of his creation. Not an additional word is needed to understand this. If all of a sudden, all bees decided to quit working and go on strike, it would surely bring about the end of the world. Harvest of plants and fruits would collapse, and all species that depend on them would be doomed to disappear in the short term. Most plants, fruits, and vegetables would disappear from supermarket shelves; Cattle would die; Wild animals that feed on prey would meet the same fate; The human species, whose food supply depends almost entirely on the generosity of the soil would also meet their end.

Bees, therefore, devote their entire lives to two primary purposes: ensuring their sustenance, the survival of their hives and the sustainability of their species, on the one hand; And, on the other hand, actively doing their part to maintain the functioning and durability of the divine creation. Bees are not different from human beings, what God requires from bees and other creatures he also requires from humans, including from you, personally. Of course, he does not expect you to go on a flower tour to pick pollen, but he expects you to provide for your family's needs, contribute to the survival of your species, and participate in the excellent functioning and preservation of his magnificent creation.

The observation of the bee teaches exciting lessons. For example, bees do not only work for food. Their efforts benefit their family (their hive or swarm) and their species, but also plants, animals, and humans. The personal benefit they draw from their hard work is only a fraction of their overall production. The time they devote to their own needs is substantially shorter than what they devote to the needs of others. In other words, bees do not live for themselves. Bees depend entirely on plants and flowers. Should flowers and fruit trees disappear, bees would immediately cease to exist.

If you are not yet convinced that bees are the greatest servants of God's Will and that they have been chosen by him to serve as living examples to those who seek to understand what God wants, follow this short demonstration.

In biblical Hebrew, the expression "Word of God" is made of the word "dabar" (רְבָד), plus the letter "Hē" (ה). "Hē" is a symbol that represents the name of God. It is the initial letter of the word "Hashem," which means "The Name." Israelites use this name instead of "God", in order to avoid pronouncing the word "God" unnecessarily and without a definite purpose. Together, dabar (רְבָד) + Hē (ה) means "Word of God." Amazingly, in Hebrew, the word that translates to "Word of God" has also two other meanings, "Bee" and "Deborah." Let's see if there is a hidden meaning there, or if it is a pure coincidence. If you are familiar with the Scripture, it is hard to believe that these associations of words have been placed there by mere coincidence.

As far as the bee is concerned, isn't this a clear hint given by the Lord to help us understand that bees have something to teach us about His Will? Now, you remember, "Ask now the beasts, and they shall teach thee; and the fowls of the air, and they shall tell thee…" (Jb 12:7–8) God wants you to imitate the bee if you want to understand what He wants you to do, and how you can do your part in the accomplishment of His Will.

Bees don't have independent lives. They can't cut their ties to the rest of the creation to alleviate their burden. Bees are, in fact, one of the multiple components of a super-organism formed by their hive, their species, and the creation. Your own life will be meaningful if only you do your part in serving the Divine Creation. Like bees, dedicate part of your daily activity to work for others, in order to ensure the sustainability of the Divine Creation, for such is his Will. This is called love, solidarity, charity, compassion, unselfishness, generosity, and it is the primary aspect of what God wants of you.

In Hebrew, the word that translates as "Word of God" also means "Bee". Is it a mere coincidence, or is it a clue sent by God so that we can understand his will?

Now, keep on walking. It's a beautiful day. Watch out and slow down! You almost crushed a poor earthworm that was crossing the sidewalk. These critters don't know the rules of the road! Take advantage of this chance encounter and ask the worm, for it probably has something to teach you.

Earthworms live underground, where they tirelessly burrow tunnels. The numerous worms that populate the underground (fertile lands may be home to more than 1,000 pounds of worms per acre), and act as the biological pistons of a giant air pump. By their body contractions, they blow surface air into the tunnels they burrow, allowing aeration and oxygenation of the soil, as well as the infiltration and retention of rainwater. The horizontal and vertical tunnels that our kind worm burrows tirelessly allow the roots of surface plants to penetrate deep into the soil.

Worms tirelessly bury deep into their tunnels organic material they find on the surface, like dead leaves, manure, or remains of dead insects. While burrowing, they swallow large amounts of soil mixed with organic matter and reject feces that are rich in nitrogen, phosphates and potassium, natural fertilizers that are at least as good as chemical ones and not harmful to the environment. Modern farmers know well how beneficial earthworms are for organic farming, and they increasingly use them.

Earthworms are at the base of multiple food chains. They feed ants, mites, centipedes, termites, snails, slugs, birds, toads, turtles, snakes, small mammals such as squirrels, mice, field rats, moles, etc. Larger mammals, such as bears, foxes, hedgehogs, wild boars, etc., also prey on them, not to mention invertebrates and beetles. In short, everyone feeds on them, including men. For some peoples, they are traditional ancestral meals of choice. If you do not eat worms yet, you may well have to start soon, because, considering the speed at which our planet is being plundered and abused, it is not unthinkable to predict that earthworms will, sooner than later, find their way on your table.

On rainy days, which they particularly like, if their many predators give them some respite, they can be seen wandering in search of other hospitable lands to create a new colony, when the size of their existing population has become too large.

Darwin, one of the first scientists to study them, wrote: "One wonders whether there are many other animals that have played in the history of the world as important a role as these creatures so imperfectly organized." The author of the theory of evolution had just witnessed the Divine Will in action but had not been interested in it more than that.

It cannot be denied that this vulgar maggot with such an unattractive appearance is, however, not only an indefatigable assistant to our farmers, to whom they render, as well as to the human species, invaluable services; And, more importantly, they also manage to work tirelessly to do their part of the accomplishment of the divine will, ensuring the excellent functioning and sustainability of the divine creation. And they never complain.

You just discovered the earthworm that frequently crosses your path. You probably used to wonder what the purpose of this pest could be. Now, after your brief conversation with the tiny critter, you know better. So, it's time you ask yourself a few questions while watching your face in your mirror, next morning. Ask yourself if you feel that you, too, are doing your part, at least as much as the humble earthworm, towards the accomplishment of the divine will and to ensure the proper functioning and the sustainability of his creation.

When you appear before God after a great Supplication or on the day of judgment, do you think that the Lord will be convinced that you are worth more or at least as much as the humble earthworm?

Worms have returned to their occupations, the sky is heavy with clouds, and it rains. Talk to the earth and the rain, they will tell you. The Bible says, "Who giveth rain upon the earth, and sendeth waters upon the fields." (Jb 5:10). This rain, without which life on earth would be impossible, God pours it upon the mountains, where the forces of gravity which God has created for the universe will rush it to the torrents; The torrents in their turn, will fill the rivers; The rivers will then feed the meager streams that bring life to the remotest parts of the earth, for the greater good of plants, animals, and men. The Bible says, "Thou visitest the earth, and waterest it: thou greatly enrichest

Ignore them and bear the consequences

it with the river of God, which is full of water: thou preparest them corn, when thou hast so provided for it. Thou waterest the ridges thereof abundantly: thou settlest the furrows thereof: thou makest it soft with showers: thou blessest the springing thereof. Thou crownest the year with thy goodness; and thy paths drop fatness. They drop upon the pastures of the wilderness: and the little hills rejoice on every side. The pastures are clothed with flocks; the valleys also are covered over with corn; they shout for joy, they also sing." (Ps 65:9–13)

To keep it always that way, so that the cries of joy and the songs resound forever for you, for your children, and the children of your children, God wants you to participate actively in the preservation of his creation, and he doesn't want anyone to hinder its proper functioning. Not doing your part in ensuring the functional operation and the everlasting sustainability of the divine creation, or thwarting its adequate functioning by inconsiderate actions, are serious offenses that will take you away from him with little hope of return if you do not remedy it without delay.

The Bible says, "For the precious things of heaven, for the dew" (Dt 33:13) God spreads water upon the fields, as do the arterial network that brings to the cells of the human body, without respite, the nutrients, oxygen, and energy that are necessary for survival and proper functioning of the cells. Should an artery clog and an organ cease to function, which could result in the death of the person. The same applies to rain and godsends. Should a farmer build a dam upstream of a river to create a water reservoir for his fields and not worry about the farms downstream, all the downstream farms will suffer from the lack of water.

That a man piles up goods and monopolizes resources for his sole benefit, beyond his own needs, without benefiting others, and the rest of the population will suffer dearly.

Observing bees, earthworms, and rain are within everyone's reach, and it is rich in teachings to understand what the Divine Will means. This is how God speaks to men. He has sown clues and answers around you in profusion, and he wants you to use the wisdom and the intelligence that he has put in you, to understand what he wants you to do. The Bible says, "Be ye therefore followers of God, as dear children." (Eph 5:1)

However, knowledge calls for responsibility, for expertise without purpose is nothing but ill-gotten wealth. Once revealed, principles impose a duty to act. An ignorant is less guilty than he who knows and yet refrains from putting his wisdom at the service of others.

Christ's advice was to question nature and animals; Jesus said, "Behold the fowls of the air: for they sow not, neither do they reap, nor gather into barns; yet your heavenly Father feedeth them." (Mt 6:26)

Look in a mirror and ask yourself if you are adequately contributing to the fulfillment of the divine will and if you are effectively participating in maintaining the proper functioning and preservation of the divine creation; at least as much as earthworms do.

When you appear before the Lord, do you think he will be convinced, in his eyes, that you are worth at least as much as the humble earthworm?

What is Divine Providence?

Divine Providence encompasses all God-given gifts that humans need to accomplish His Will and preserve his creation; That is all the graces God provides to his creatures, so they can do their part to ensure the everlasting sustainability of his beautiful work. It's in the diligent care of God for his great nature and creatures that providential grace is revealed. When God gives a purpose to his creatures, he does not merely assign a mission, then leaves them to fend for themselves and find the means to complete this duty; God always gives the means necessary for the accomplishment of this mission. To achieve the end, he provides the means. The Bible says: "Upholding all things by the word of his power." (Heb 1:3) God wants each of his creatures to devote themselves to fulfilling his will, the good one, and the wicked, the righteous, and the unjust, the believer, and the atheist. Christ said that "God maketh his sun to rise on the evil and on the good, and sendeth rain on the just and on the unjust." (Mt 5:45)

The everlasting sustainability of his Creation is the mission he entrusts to each of his creatures, and divine providence is the means he gives them to achieve this end. Ensuring the everlasting sustainability of the Creation implies respect for the land and ecological ecosystems, protection and respect of animals, safeguarding natural resources, as well as the duty to maintain yourself in good health through an appropriate lifestyle. The divine will also imply our responsibility to transmit to future generations the Divine Creation, in the same state as when we received it.

Divine Providence, it's daily bread, happiness, and prosperity. When Christ said, "Give us this day our daily bread," (Mt 6:11) he was referring to the Divine Providence, for if providence were missing, life could not continue. It's the divine providence that allowed the Hebrews to survive during the forty years of their journey through the desert; A desert so arid and inhospitable, that the people of Israel would never have survived without the divine providence. The Bible says, "The children of Israel did eat manna forty years." (Ex 16:35) God sent the manna, a providential food, to the Hebrews, for forty years, until they finally reached the land of Canaan, which God had promised to give to Abraham and his descendants.

Divine providence is physical nourishment for the body, but also spiritual food for the mind. Therefore, the Scripture is also Divine Providence. The Bible says, "Man doth not live by bread only, but by every word that proceedeth out of the mouth of the Lord doth man live." (Dt 8:3) For those who have understood it, providential grace is also one way that leads to sanctification and salvation. The Bible says, "[God] make you perfect in every good work to do his Will." (Heb 13:21)

How Does Divine Providence Work?

God sends His gifts through his creations and His creatures, which continuously interact and form a complex network of living beings working together with the same purpose. None of the divine gifts reaches its recipient directly without having first transited through the complex web of God's servants. Thus, as an example, when God wants to give his blessing to plants, he entrusts bees to accomplish his will. Bees fly from one flower to another, and they put in the pistil of female flowers the pollen they collected from male flowers. This is called pollination. Thus, the providential action of the bee ensures bountiful harvests. God wants every one of his creatures to participate in his organization network, for the good of all. And if you receive his blessings and graces through the bees, there may be no doubt that it is God who sent them to you. Who cares about bees when purchasing fruits or when eating an apple? No one! However, whenever you eat a fruit, remember with humble gratitude that it's thanks to the relentless work of the bees in contributing to the fulfillment of the will of God.

Ignore them and bear the consequences

Confirmation by the Spirit

The Lord said, "I will put my law in their inward parts, and write it in their hearts." (Jer 31:33) The psalmist confirmed: "The law of his God is in his heart;" (Ps 37:31) And "Who hath put wisdom in the inward parts? or who hath given understanding to the heart?" (Jb 38:36) When God gave Moses his commandments, he said to him, "These words, which I command thee this day, shall be in thine heart." (Dt 6:6) And the Bible says again: "There is a spirit in man: and the inspiration of the Almighty giveth them understanding." (Jb 32: 8)

The Bible contains many occurrences of words or expressions that refer to "spirit." Divine Spirit, Breath of God, Divine Light, Spirit of man, intelligence, and wisdom. Job reveals that the Lord has endowed each of His creatures with "spirit" that allows them to live, to provide for their needs, and to ensure the survival of their species; "Doth the hawk fly by thy wisdom, and stretch her wings toward the south?" (Jb 39:26) "Doth the eagle mount up at thy command, and make her nest on high?" (Jb 39:27) It is certainly not by the acts nor by the will of man that animals act as they ought. Animals know what they ought to do to live, to hunt, to feed and shelter their offspring. They don't need to be taught in these matters. The spirit they have received, like all members of their species, allows them to live according to the specific rules of their species.

Could animals live if they had not been endowed with spirit? Certainly not! They would be no different than the stones of the way. This suggests that spirit is the essence of life, although it's not only the essence of life. Spirit that abides in animals contains an owner's manual of life, as well as a panoply of useful instruments specific to each species, instinct, preconditioned reflexes, memory, that allows animals to live autonomously, in conformity with the specificities of their species.

Man, too, have received the spirit specific to their species, and in addition, they have also received intelligence and wisdom. The Bible says, "Who hath put wisdom in the inward parts? or who hath given understanding to the heart?" (Jb 38:36) And "I have filled him with the spirit of God, in wisdom, and in understanding, and in knowledge, and in all manner of workmanship." (Ex 31:3) Without the breath of the Almighty, which gives intelligence to the mind of man, men would not be different from animals. Here, we ought to distinguish between "spirit" and "Spirit." The word written with a lowercase initial refers to the spirit of man, which in all respects is similar to that of animals. It is the spirit of the flesh and of life, that allows living beings to be, to live, and to ensure the sustainability of their species. The Bible says, "That which befalleth the sons of men befalleth beasts; even one thing befalleth them: as the one dieth, so dieth the other; yea, they have all one breath; so that a man hath no preeminence above a beast: for all is vanity." (Eccl 3:19)

The word written with an uppercase initial letter refers to the Divine Spirit, the breath of the Lord, which gives intelligence to the mind and causes humans to no longer belong in the animal species and to elevate themselves to become what the Lord wants them to be. The Lord said, "I will put my Spirit in you." (Ez 36:27, 37:14) This Spirit that God put into man is a fragment of his own Divine Spirit. The Bible says again: "The anointing which ye have received of him abideth in you, and ye need not that any man teach you." (1 Jn 2:27)

In the book of Ezekiel, the Lord reveals how he intends to communicate with man, thanks to His Spirit, which he put in them so that they may fulfill his Will. The Lord God said, "I have poured out my spirit upon the house of Israel." (Ez 39:29; Is 44: 3) Therefore, thanks to the Spirit you may know his will. The Bible says, "In thy light shall we see light." (Ps 36:9)

Ignore them and bear the consequences

Understanding the Divine Will is the first step toward spiritual fulfillment, as well as the indispensable prerequisite of supplication, for seeking to understand what is the Will of God means seeking God himself.

Law #3
The Law of Sanctification

"Ye shall be holy: for I the LORD your God am holy." (Lv 19:2)

Holiness and Sanctification

Holiness defines the absolute perfection of God. This word does not apply to man, even to the holiest among them, for the sanctity of man cannot compare with the Holiness of God. Sanctification is the Divine Consecration for those who love God with all their hearts and who engage with high energy in the quest for God's Will.

Holiness, for man, is a God-given grace. Those who receive this blessing or sanctification are distinguished by the Lord. God singles them out from the rest of the human crowd by sanctifying them and designating them as holy among men and chosen by God.

To be sanctified, you ought to want it fervently, and you ought to love God with all your heart, with all your soul, and with all your strength. More important, you must be called, and when your time comes, you ought to be prepared and know how to elevate your soul towards him.

In your life, you have undoubtedly devoted much of your time to improve your prosperity and material comfort for yourself and your family. Unconsciously but inevitably, you have moved away from the way of God. Your past negligence or indifference has slowly led you on a slippery path that, in terms of your relationship with God is not leading you anywhere. Now, you realize that you must stop drifting and take action for your redemption. You long for returning to God, but you don't know where to start and how to do it. You were holy at birth, but you gradually renounced your innate qualities, purity, and innocence, and you have inevitably moved away from the Lord. You perceive the divine presence on the horizon, and you would like to draw nearer to him before he disappears, but the dinghy that carries you no longer responds to your control. After having sailed for so long across the oceans, its rudder is no longer responding, and its hull is full of barnacles that prevent the boat from moving forward. As if you were carried away by a frail raft, aimless and without direction, at the mercy of the currents, going somewhere except to where you would like to go. You have waited too long to start worrying and to put an end to this bad dream; but, it's not a dream. You look like a terrified lamb facing a pack of hungry wolves. Suffering, anguish perhaps, have prompted you to ask yourself the right questions and take action.

Blinded by the fog, you fear to cross the street because although you can't see the traffic, you feel the roar of the speeding cars coming from the right and left. You had always trusted your eyes, but you can no longer count on them. You clearly need help, and you turn to God, hoping that he will hear you and that he will, in your favor, make a miracle. But, the Bible says, "Then shall they call upon me, but I will not answer; they shall seek me early, but they shall not find me." (Prv 1:28).

As it sometimes happens while driving, you realize that you

are heading in the wrong direction. These things also happen in life. You plan to go somewhere, you think how to get there, but after you have driven for an hour, you realize that you are on the wrong road. It's never too late to backtrack and get in the right direction. God willing, with strong personal will and determination, you will succeed. Sanctification is the process of transformation through purification, which allows you to reconnect with God; Ask Him for help with prayers and supplications. The Bible says, "Teach me good judgment and knowledge: for I have believed thy commandments." (Ps 119: 66).

The answer is in the Scripture. God will not forsake you. "They that know thy name will put their trust in thee: for thou, Lord, hast not forsaken them that seek thee." (Ps 9:10) But don't wait, for life is too short to keep on erring, even for a single day. You take the risk of not having enough time to find the right path in the labyrinth of life. But, since you are reading these lines, it means the fire is still alive in your heart, and your will to act is authentic and ardent. With God's help, you will reach your goal by prayer and supplication.

An effective supplication is not a poetic text with pretty words and gracious style effects that begins with "Lord" and ends with "Amen." The choice of words and their profusion, the subtlety of style, the grammatical syntax and spelling accuracy, do not affect a Supplication's efficiency. Had it been otherwise, supplications by writers, journalists, and all those whose job is to write would be answered much more often than those by blue collars. Fortunately, this is not the case. The weight of the words, the awe of elegant figures of style, and the literary quality of your supplications are not likely to influence the divine generosity in your favor. What matters when you go to God is the purity of your soul, the sincerity of your approach, and the intensity of your enthusiasm.

Ignore them and bear the consequences

The Holiness Requirement

God is holy because he is absolute perfection. The Saints of religions are men who have distinguished themselves from other men by living exemplary lives according to the way of God, in conforming with his law and commandments, and who have done their part in working for fulfilling God's Will. However, God alone has the power to recognize that a man is holy.

God wants you to be holy not by becoming, like him, absolute perfection, a divine quality that humans cannot attain, but by becoming as blessed as you can be, through sanctification. By distinguishing yourself from the rest of the human crowd; By leading an exemplary and spiritual life, in respect of his laws and commandments; And above all, by working continuously to fulfill his Will.

The Lord said, "Ye shall be holy: for I the Lord your God am holy." (Lv 19:2). This verse is not merely an invitation to sanctification. It contains a powerful message you should not ignore: God wants you to become holy. This requirement is not a commandment like all others, which you know well for having read them often, but which you forget to abide by, for perhaps you have not grasped their meaning and importance. The Ten Commandments, you know them by heart, for having heard them a hundred times, and since you are reading this guide, I will bet you killed no one, you do not rob old ladies, and adultery is not your daily bread. But, perhaps, have you relegated this crucial decree that is the divine requirement of holiness on the waiting list of your concerns, to reflect on it later? Well, no! Know if you fail to make progress towards your sanctification, you will postpone your chance of getting closer to God.

This requirement of sanctification implies the observance and respect of all divine decrees, for God said, "Shall ye observe all my statutes, and all my judgments, and do them: I am the Lord."

(Lv 19:37) The holiness requirement concerns everyone. It is not addressed only to the clergy, or to any category of population, for God instructed Moses to make this commandment known "to all the congregation of the children of Israel" (Lv 19:2); That is, to the whole population.

Would it come to you to attend a private party with dirty hands and neglected outfits? Have you ever thought of attending the wedding of your boss's daughter in neglected clothing? So, how could you imagine approaching God when you are not neatened up and personable?

The requirement of sanctification also implies that you accept being God's servant and recognize the Lord, creator of the universe, earth and heaven and all living creatures, as your only God. The Bible says, "Hear, O Israel: The Lord our God is one Lord." (Dt 6:4)

This divine requirement is justified by the sanctity of God Himself. He asks no one to be as perfect as he is nor to act like him, but simply to be holy as a man can be, for he doesn't hook up with those who have gone astray and who don't fight to keep vice, corruption, and sin at bay. It is legitimate that he wants those who wish to get closer to him to be like him, spotless.

All earthly life has an end, a deliverance that allows the soul to free itself from the body and from everything else that holds it down here. The Bible says: "He that is dead is freed from sin." (Rom 6:7) Sanctification is the assurance of eternal life that begins here and continues up there. It is a deliverance that takes place during your lifetime and helps you get rid of everything that runs contrary to the Divine Spirit that abides in you. "Sanctify yourselves therefore, and be ye holy." (Lv 20:7) "But as he which hath called you is holy, so be ye holy" (1 Pt 1:15)

The word "holy" used in the Bible means both "set apart," that is, "separated" from the majority of humans; And "pure," that is, honorable, upright. In this light, you will better understand what this biblical verse means: "Come out from among them, and be ye separate, saith the Lord, and touch not the unclean thing; and I will receive you." (2 Cor 6:17) Do not hook up with those who have chosen the wrong path. Separate yourself from them and be pure, for, the Scripture says, "God hath not called us unto uncleanness, but unto holiness." (1 Thes 4:7).

Beware, he who does not ardently desire it should not expect to become sanctified. Although sanctification is a divine requirement, it is not universally sought. Some prefer to live as they please and try above all not to complicate their lives. They are convinced that pursuing sanctification is a burden they can well do without to live happily. If, like them, you think that pursuing sanctification is an unnecessary complication and a waste of time, don't make your life too complicated, enjoy ignorance, close this book and instead read a good thriller!

Pursuing sanctification is a choice like all the choices available to you and will continue to be available to you in every moment of your life. Decisions are like the small adjustments right or left that you give reflexively to the steering wheel while driving, to correct the course of your car and to ensure that it doesn't deviate from its way. Forget to rectify your vehicle when needed, and you will end up in the ditch. If you elect to seek sanctification for yourself, you must do whatever it takes to make it so. In conclusion, sanctification is not just a step towards fulfilling the divine will; Sanctification "is" the divine will.

Sanctification is the assurance of an eternal life which begins down here and continues up there.

How to Become Holy

Consider God's requirement of holiness as a personal moral obligation that you must commit yourself to achieving, with a firm determination and all your energy, in your life. You will choose from among all the alternatives available to you, the one that seems to you the most suitable to respond to the divine ordinance, "be holy." The mere fact of committing yourself to fulfill this divine decree will allow you to deepen your relationship with God and your chances of being, one day, admitted into God's intimate circle.

Sanctification requires a sustained effort. However, there is no other alternative. If you think the price to pay is too high for you, try ignorance.

To embark on the path to sanctification is to put God before you and to associate him to all decisions and choices you'll make in your life, that will remain as your spiritual milestones alongside your road to sanctification. The more you progress on this path, the more you'll be drawn to him.

You have completed much of the trip, and you are homing in on your goal. Don't give up; persist!

"Wash you, make you clean; put away the evil of your doings from before mine eyes; cease to do evil." (Is 1:16) This verse summarizes the precepts of sanctification in simple words. If you don't succeed and have no more confidence in yourself, and if you struggle with anxiety and depression, that means you lead your life as you please, according to your own will or lack of it, in contempt of God's will. That also means that the biblical principles of sanctification are unfamiliar to you. When things go wrong for you, stop looking for causes elsewhere than in yourself. Don't shift the responsibility of your failures onto others. Instead, recognize that you have strayed far from the way of God. However, well-diagnosed ailments are well on the way to being healed. But the Scripture says "to him that knoweth to

Ignore them and bear the consequences

do good, and doeth it not, to him it is sin." (Jas 4:17).

Etch in your memory the biblical principles developed in this guide. Read them again and again. Endeavor to comprehend their meaning and make these principles your way of life, for they will guide you to the divine light. Open your mind to the good influence of these simple words and, each day, adopt one precept and make it the object of your reflection and study of that day. Do it with a critical mind and ask yourself how you may have overlooked these divine principles, how you got away from them, and how you could get back in the game, says the Bible. "Let not sin therefore reign in your mortal body." (Rom 6:12).

The word "Saint" only applies to the Lord. It is often said that God is good, generous, omnipotent, tolerant, merciful, and so on. Those epithets better suit man, and when applied to God, they give the Lord an anthropomorphic image that does not suit him well. They are overloaded with emotional feelings, the same emotional states that make a man a weak and fragile being. But the Lord is not weakened by emotions. If that were the case, be worried. God is holy, and this is why he wants you to be sanctified. Any epithet added to the word "saint" when associated with God is useless, excessive, and inappropriate, for it only attenuates the essence of the word "Saint." To be holy is to be perfect. However, man will never attain the same holiness as the Lord. Getting rid of excess emotional feelings will help you turn your back on the constraining urges that poison your life, and resist temptations; You will gain in integrity, and you will be on your way to sanctification.

Like everyone else, you're meant to be holy. However, you must take the steps that will lead you to sanctification, on your own volition, Paul said. "And that ye put on the new man, which after God is created in righteousness and true holiness." (Eph 4:24). The Bible says: "I am the Lord which sanctify you." (Lv 20:8) So, it is the Lord who will decide whether your journey has been sincere and whether you deserve to be sanctified.

Praise the Lord and acknowledge that the Lord is your only God. The Bible says: "There is none other God but one." (1 Cor 8:4) Love and worship the Lord with all the love and all the enthusiasm which you are capable of; Strive to resemble the image of God, "God created man in his own image." (Gn 1:27) making sure you never tarnish this image.

At first sight, man is but an animal like the others. Few things set him apart from other animals, except that among the plethora of living beings that God created, man is the only creature God created in his image. Therefore, you may well say that man is not different from animals, yet, this animal has been given a purpose that transcends their life, that of finding their holy model. And, to fulfill this purpose, humans have been endowed with all the tools they need.

The First Commandment

The Scriptures reveal that when Moses taught his people the word he had received from God, he said, "Hear, O Israel: The Lord our God is one Lord: And thou shalt love the Lord thy God with all thine heart, and with all thy soul, and with all thy might." (Dt 6:4) And when a scribe asked Christ what was, according to him, the first commandment of the Lord, Christ replied by citing this same verse: "The first of all the commandments is, Hear, O Israel; The Lord, our God, is one Lord: And thou shalt love the Lord thy God with all thy heart, and with all thy soul, and with all thy mind, and with all thy strength: this is the first commandment." (Mk 12:29) The most significant accomplishment in a man's life is to belong to the Lord. However, to become God's own possession requires your total and unconditional commitment to the one and only God, and by this worshipful commitment, you must engage in a continuously renewed pattern of adoration and worship.

You wonder what it means to love God with all your heart, with all your soul, and with all your strength. Love God in this way, and you'll be convinced that even if your doubts and hardships do not disappear on the spot, God will help you to perceive the bad moments of your life from another perspective and to understand that your difficulties of the moment are but slight transient afflictions. The Bible says: "Our light affliction, which is but for a moment, worketh for us a far more exceeding and eternal weight of glory." (2 Cor 4:17) Your afflictions requiring emergency relief and immediate admission to ICU will be soon forgotten, for you will understand how much God loves you. God loves you, and He wants you to love Him. The Bible says: "God is love; and he that dwelleth in love dwelleth in God, and God in him." (1 Jn 4:16) However, it's up to you to make the first move, for God always loved you, even since before you were conceived, "We love him, because he first loved us." (1 Jn 4:19).

The Divine Grace

Grace means undeserved or unjustified favor. Grace is granted by God in His sole discretion. Kings, sovereigns, heads of states, governors, have always enjoyed similar, sovereign rights, such as the right to declare war against a foreign country, the right to create new laws, to levy taxes, the right to mint coins, and issue banknotes. These rights are called sovereigns because they belong exclusively to monarchs or heads of States. This is also true for the authority to pardon, which rulers, heads of states, and governors still have today in many countries. The power to grant amnesty allows a leader to give full or partial pardon to a person who was tried and convicted and has exhausted all legal appeals.

The sovereigns, of whom some said that they had themselves been placed on the throne by the grace of God, could thus spare a convict sentenced to the gallows, or reduce the sentence of an unfortunate convicted of pilfering, without having to justify their decision. Divine grace responds to the same principle of justice when all remedies at law have been exhausted, and there is no more recourse.

God has the privilege to grant his grace to all his children, with no restriction, without distinction of race or origin, to believers and unbelievers, to the good or to the bad guys, according to the Bible. "He [God] maketh his sun to rise on the evil and on the good, and sendeth rain on the just and on the unjust." (Mt 5:45)

What Does "In His Image" Mean?

The expression "in his image" does not refer to a supposed or implied anthropomorphic depiction of God, as a mirror may reflect your image. Some mistakenly represent God with anthropomorphic traits because they misunderstand this expression. The expression "in His image", on the contrary, refers to an assortment of divine qualities which God has endowed man, and man alone with among all his creatures, the spirit, mindfulness, the power of introspection, and of being able to question himself, of seeking who God is and what divine will means; and the ability to understand what the purpose of life is; And, more important, the ability to distinguish good from evil and right from wrong. All this makes sense to the expression "in his own image," as it is understood in the Scriptures, "Ye shall be as gods, knowing good and evil." (Gn 3:5) "Ye are gods" (Ps 82: 6, Is 41:23, Jn 10:34) You are supposed to know the difference between "god" as it appears in Gn 3:5, and "God," our Lord, the one and only God.

Ignore them and bear the consequences

Sanctification Through Imitation

God wants your desire for sanctification to result from your own free will and not a simple act of obedience. Therefore, sanctification is an option, and it's up to you to choose and to commit yourself to it. The choice is solely yours. If you are unsure of the direction you should go to, it is that your level of spiritual consciousness is not mature yet. Take time to understand. Ask your parents, friends, spiritual counselor, because once you have taken the commitment of becoming sanctified, you'll be obligated to comply.

God doesn't force you to become holy, and you know for a fact that he always keeps his promises. However, when you enter into a covenant with him on your own volition, he wants you to respect it.

The wording of the divine commandment seems to suggest that God wants you to imitate him (Lv 19: 2). This verse, which effectively invites to imitate, could also imply "be generous, for I am generous," or "be righteous, for I am righteous." Sanctification through imitation helps to create a unique personal relationship with your Creator, which is the central theme and the guiding thread of supplication, from the initial awareness of the first commandment that reveals how God should be loved and worshipped and the need to become God's high possession, until the sublime moment when you'll be admitted into his presence.

Where to Start

So, your decision is made. You are determined to begin the journey that will lead you to sanctification, an essential step for those who want to get closer to God. The effort is within your reach. Each one progresses according to his own means, level of education, propensity for understanding what God wants, or their proficiency in Bible studies. To achieve sanctification, you must focus on three specific areas: your relationships with others; Your relationship with your ego; And your relationship with God.

When you have established harmonious and honest relationships with others, with your ego, and with God, your biblically transformed and sublimated self will become supplication in an endogenous manner. Then, God will know that the purpose you have chosen of your own free will is to become His servant, to fulfill His will, and live according to his way. Instead of "servant," the word "partner" would be more accurate, for "partner" better reflects that you have entered into a covenant with the Lord and that you have agreed to work closely with him for the accomplishment of his Divine Will. From then on, God will let you know the mission he has assigned to you, and he will give you all that you need to succeed.

As for your own personal needs, words will become superfluous to express them, for your life will have become like a Supplication. You will be holy. Those who are admitted into the intimate circle of God's chosen ones have nothing more to ask. All their needs are satisfied.

When you have become God's partner through a covenant you have entered into with the Lord, and when you have agreed to study His Will, you'll work closely with Him, for the accomplishment of that goal. From then on, God will let you know the mission He has assigned to you, and He will give you everything you need to succeed. As for your own personal needs, words will become superfluous to express them, for, thanks to your new status with God, your life will have become like a Supplication. You will be holy. Those who are admitted into the intimate circle of God's chosen ones have nothing more to ask. All their needs are satisfied, like birds, which need not ask, to sow, and or to reap, yet the Lord feeds them. "Behold the fowls of the air: for

Ignore them and bear the consequences

they sow not, neither do they reap nor gather into barns; yet your heavenly Father feedeth them" (Mt 6:26).

A. Your Relationships with Others

Most, if not all, of our choices and decisions, are motivated by selfish desires, whereas they ought to have been motivated by altruism and empathy. Relationships with others are the source of all frustrations and bitterness, which poison lives and blacken souls. However, it is, paradoxically, in this area, it is easier to carry out the work of sanctification, as the obstacles you must overcome are easily identifiable.

There are three parties to any relationship with others, and you are one party. The second party will sometimes be the others at large, all the others; At other times, the second party might be a group of individuals with a common denominator, a category of people put together under the same label, for they are not close enough to you so you can distinguish them individually; Other times, the second party might have a name, a face, and a story, and you could know them personally, a relative, a friend, a business acquaintance, a store owner in your neighborhood, a coworker, a neighbor, etc.

The third party is God, for God is directly affected by your relationships with others, as an offense to others is also an offense against God. Conversely, being generous amounts to praising God, according to the Bible. "He that oppresseth the poor reproacheth his Maker: but he that honoureth him hath mercy on the poor." (Prv 14:31).

The definition of "the other" includes the stranger who lives among you. Although he might be sitting next to you, you could consider him to be far away from you, for his manners and customs differ from yours. This difference in which you lock him up gives him, on the contrary, access to a privileged status that of all the poor and oppressed, the standing of protected souls of the Lord. This verse is a warning to those who would be tempted to oppress the needy or to abuse the stranger, for in acting negatively against them, it's God himself you'll be offending.

Not only do aliens ought to be considered your equals at law, but, you have to give them the same level of love, care, and empathy as you give to your friends, and to members of your community. You must give them the same benefits and the same treatment and love them as you do to your best friends. In international trade and economic relations, the "most favored nation" is a status or level of treatment accorded by developed countries to developing countries. Great economic powers grant to some developing countries the benefits of the so-called "most favored nation" clause. When added in an international treaty, this provision extends to beneficiary countries the same advantages as those already accorded to the most favored countries. This is what God wants you to do. God wants you to extend to aliens the same level of care and empathy you grant to your best friends. The Bible says: "He that loveth not knoweth not God; for God is love." (1 Jn 4:8) It is impossible to love God without loving one's neighbor (1 Jn 4:20).

Some biblical authors emphasize their message using a particular figure of style, which consists of a rapid crescendo progression of three or four words. In Lv 19, this progression begins with general themes. "Ye shall not steal, neither deal falsely, neither lie one to another." (Lv 19:11) They are then followed by social and economic themes involving collective responsibility: the exploitation of the humble, the working people, the needy, or the infirm, as in. "Thou shalt not defraud thy neighbour, neither rob him: the wages of him that is hired shall not abide with thee all night until the morning. Thou shalt not curse the deaf, nor put a stumbling block before the blind, but shalt fear thy God: I am the Lord." (Lv 19:13–14) Then, in Lv 19:15, it evokes the corruption and undue influence that the better-off can exert over the courts to the detriment of the humblest, "Ye shall do no unrighteousness in judgment: thou shalt not respect the person of the poor, nor honor the person of the mighty: but in righteousness shalt thou judge thy neighbour."

It finally ends with the hatred that corrodes the heart of men, and vengeance, daughter of hatred, as in "Thou shalt not hate thy brother in thine heart" (Lv 19:17) "Thou shalt not avenge, nor bear any grudge against the children of thy people" (Lv 19:18) With the supreme commandment, verse 18 ends in an apotheosis. "Thou shalt love thy neighbour as thyself" (Lv 19:18, Mt 19:19, 22:39, Mk 12:31, Lk 10:27, Rom 13 9: Gal 5:14, Jas 2:8)

This dramatic progression, which culminates in chapter 19 of Leviticus by the commandment to love one's neighbor, gives to relations with others a dimension that goes beyond simple social, economic, or legal justice and transcends the love for God through loving others, central precepts of the Divine Will.

The Bible says, "Let us not therefore judge one another anymore: but judge this rather, that no man put a stumbling block or an occasion to fall in his brother's way." (Rom 14:13)

Relations with others are governed by two essential precepts; on the one hand, the Golden Rule and its reversed version, and its corollary, the Royal Law.

The Golden Rule

To someone who asked him to explain in a few words the Law of Moses, the sage Hillel, whose active years have spanned over 40 years (30 BCE - 10 CE), replied: "Do not do unto others what you wouldn't want that someone do unto you. This is all the Law, as for the rest, these are but commentaries."

The golden rule is a unilateral commitment where the first party agrees to give something to the second party and to receive no payment of any kind in return. The golden rule often appears in the Old Testament and the New Testament, and it concerns all the fundamental biblical precepts that deal with the love of neighbor.

The Bible says, "Who so stoppeth his ears at the cry of the poor, he also shall cry himself, but shall not be heard." (Prv 21:13) "As thou hast done, it shall be done unto thee" (Ob 15) "Therefore all things whatsoever ye would that men should do to you, do ye even so to them: for this is the law and the prophets." (Mt 7:12)

The golden rule is a personal commitment that binds you morally and irrevocably. It means you have voluntarily committed to treating others as you would like them to treat you. Those who might think they can escape the obligations imposed by such a commitment only morally binding must think twice.

Although they are not likely to have to appear before a judge for their failure to honor their obligation, they should remember that God is a party in all relationships with others. Therefore, if they escape the justice of men, they will still have to face God's judgment.

The Royal Law

The royal law is about the love of neighbor. The Bible says that the Lord commanded Moses to teach this law to all the children of Israel, "Thou shalt love thy neighbor as thyself." (Lv 19:18, Gal 5:14, Mt 22:39) for all men are brothers and, as creatures of God, they are equal before God, our Lord, the one and only God. This law is a little more demanding than the Golden Rule, of which it is the consequence. The golden rule says you have to behave with the others as you would want the others to act with you. As per the Royal Law, although the Golden Rule prevents conflicts, it does not go far enough to satisfy the divine requirement. God wants you to love your neighbor. He not only wants you to commit yourself to the highest standard of behavior towards him, as the Golden Rule demands, but he also wants you to love him with a strength and willpower capable of dominating your own egoism and self-centeredness.

Altruism is the opposite of egoism and egocentrism. It is a benevolent inclination towards others based on the love of the neighbor, which pushes to privilege the well-being of others to the detriment of one's own well-being. When one faces misfortune, the instinctive impulse to act first for oneself is ignored, so others may be helped first. The verb love implies here loving your neighbor in a non-passive way, actively bringing your love to him. The Bible says, "Thou shalt love thy neighbour as thyself." (Gal 5:14, Lv 19:18, Mt 22:39). The focus is on the attitude you must have towards others, not how you feel about others. To love one's neighbor, one must not do anything harmful against him, despising him, ignoring him, lessening him, or calling him a bad name.

Love of neighbor is not only towards your fellow men but especially, towards those who differ from you. The Bible says: "The stranger that dwelleth with you shall be unto you as one born among you, and thou shalt love him as thyself" (Lv 19:34) To love one's neighbor is not to recognize oneself in the other, but to recognize and accept his difference, which makes him the "other," while being, like yourself, a unique being in search of love and recognition. It is also to want to do good to the other in a disinterested manner. To love the other means to listen to him and to show him he is not indifferent to you; Giving him without him having to ask; Ensuring he never feels lonely. However, it also means making him understand that he too has something to give.

Indifference amounts to killing the other by not recognizing his existence. Indifference and exclusion are synonymous with murder. Murder causes immediate death, whereas the absence of interest kills slowly, but just as surely. Both are significant sins because not conforming to a commandment amount to doing the opposite, like not doing good, amounts to doing evil.

You owe to your fellow men all the respect and dignity they deserve, for, as Prophet Malachi said "Have we not all one father? hath not one God created us?" (Mal 2:10).

Love of neighbor is not an end. It is, above all, an essential prerequisite for fulfilling the divine requirement of holiness because the love of one's neighbor is the first step to becoming holy. You will achieve this by a daily work of sanctification that will elevate you towards the divine light, and bring you closer to God. The Bible says, "If ye fulfill the royal law according to the scripture, Thou shalt love thy neighbour as thyself, ye do well" (Jas 2: 8).

To love your neighbor, who, like you, was created in God's image, is to love God. Is it so hard to love God? Is it so hard to love? If you are capable of loving, place your neighbor before you, as to show him you love him, you must put him first, before yourself.

Remember that each party in any relationship has the power to influence and transform this relationship and make it evolve into a warm and friendly relationship, keep it as is and not change anything to it, or even make it turn sour; Each one can keep the connection distant and neutral, although courteous. Each party can privilege impersonal and remote interactions, and keep them at a minimum.

One or two centuries ago, people traveled little. They were born in a village or a neighborhood, attended the same school and the same church, married a neighbor, and were buried in the same cemetery. Childhood friends used to remain friends for the rest of their lives, and neighbors were often related members of the same large family. When someone met a new face, the first question was to ask him if he was the son of Jenny, the baker's daughter, or the son of Liz, the seamstress. People shared a mutual history and a few family ties. All that remained to do was to renew ties never totally broken. Today, more efforts are needed to create or maintain new relationships with others.

If neither side takes the initiative, there is no hope of improving the climate of a relationship. So, you'd better take this initiative yourself, if you want to live in a better world, if only within the microcosm of your immediate universe. However, you have issues to solve before you devote yourself to do it with some chances of success. Some of these problems are inherent to yourself. They are not very difficult to answer if you have the will.

Nowadays, people move more, and they go further. They easily forget their childhood friends for they are quickly replaced by the new friends they meet along the way. Virtual friends found on social networks on the Internet replace the old friends, with whom they had much to share.

It becomes necessary and urgent to recreate human contacts and personal relationships. What prevents this relationship from being created is such a stupid and silly thing you won't want to admit it. And yet! If an elegant young man approaches you to talk to you, you will not be reluctant to answer him and to speak with him, without suspicion and even with some pleasure. But if you are being approached by a sloppy man with messy hair, you would have some reluctance, even some wariness, to let him get too close to you, and you will have no desire to engage in conversation with him—no need to go any further. What prevents you from approaching people with whom you might have had a good relationship, it's this unfavorable a priori that stops you.

When you learn of this, you make the efforts required to

correct it. But as archaeologists working on excavation sites know it, after the superficial layer of dust, lower layers are harder to dig through, because they comprise rock. Digging deeper into yourself, you might well discover that layers and layers of resentment, bitterness, desire for vengeance, lust, envy, iniquity, and hate remain hidden. These feelings buried deep in your heart are sometimes discernible, but more often, they stay hidden deep within your being, and they prevent you from having healthy relationships with others.

These flaws, for they are flaws, make of you a pariah, an untouchable, for even if you are not aware of it, they remain in you, deep within your subconscious mind. They influence and poison your relationships with others and your relationship with God. The existence of these flaws is not something new for you. You knew they existed, and although you conveniently hid them from your sight, you did not delete them. They are still there, like intestinal cancer you can't see, but which nevertheless gnaws at you. They can reappear on the surface. You have to eliminate them at all costs. You must extirpate from your soul those poisons that undermine you and which prevent you from having healthy relationships with others and with God.

When you get to this point, and I strongly hope you will, you must still search deep in yourself to find out and wipe out hidden stains, for everybody has skeletons in their closet, which have been locked up there, by an unconscious will to keep them buried in the depth of their consciousness.

I pray with you, and I pray for you, that you and all those who endeavor to do the hard work needed to get there, succeed, with God's help. Amen!

Ignore them and bear the consequences

B. Your Relationship with your Self

As in relationship with others, there are three parties in connection with yourself, God, yourself, and your ego. You must take enough distance with your ego to examine it and criticize with no trace of narcissism and, above all, without complacency.

Your relationship with your ego has a decisive influence both on the quality of your relationships with others and on the link you would like to establish with God. How could you hope to build a relationship with God if you don't even dare to build a relationship with the person facing you every morning when you look at your mirror? This mirror, with which you have an implicit and discreet conversation, is a faithful friend, because, by sending you an accurate picture without alterations of your appearance at the jump of the bed, it alerts you on what you must rectify to your outfit to make you presentable. A comb, a smile on your face, a drop of fragrance, a fitting tie or a well-applied lipstick, and you have become another person—a social person, ready to please, to seduce, to be accepted, and above all, to increase the circle of your relations.

Alas, this faithful mirror doesn't give you an image of your inner being. You may think it doesn't matter because nobody can see what's in you, but you are wrong. An attentive person can well discern what you hide within yourself, and even if no one pays attention to you, God looks at you from above. Your look, the unconscious body language of your face, your attitude can betray more secrets than you can imagine. But God sees you as you are. So, absent a specialized mirror that remains to be invented, to verify that what is in you is conforming to what you want to be, try to see yourself as God sees you.

See Yourself as God Sees You

The image reflected in your mirror is not really you; it is only part of yourself, the external representation of your body. Your soul is absent from your image in the mirror. This is not how God sees you. When he looks at you, God does not seek to know if you are well-groomed and if you make a good impression. When God looks at you, everything about you appears to him, even what's hidden. Your naked soul, without artifice or makeup, is visible to him. He sees it as it is, whereas, for you, your ego is only a famous unknown, a stranger, of whom you are not even sure whether he is hostile or friendly with you.

If you want to see yourself as God sees you, move away from your mirror, dive deep inside of yourself and observe your ego with honesty and humility and above all without complacency.

It doesn't mean you should fall into contemplation in front of the beautiful image of your ego you may have discovered. But don't slip into depression because you would have so much liked to see another picture of yourself than the one you just saw. You ought to observe with a critical eye as if you were observing another being than yourself. The image of oneself always appears either too beautiful, if one is euphoric, or ugly if one is depressed. How could you progress? It is essential to see you as you are, as God sees you, to advance towards sanctification. You have to get to know your ego, as if it were another person, without judgment.

Even if you think you have never sinned, you are not necessarily living the life God wants you to live. You might simply be like a horseman on a galloping horse suddenly stung by a wasp. The ride is not unpleasant if you like to gallop, but you do not know where your horse is leading you. It's time to calm your mount and regain control. You might realize that he was leading you straight to a cliff. In real life, it is the same. One day, you have to stop this crazy race, take a deep breath, and ask yourself if you are on the right track and if you can keep your life under control. Ask yourself who you are, what you look like, whether the image of yourself is in conformity with, or on the contrary, is far away from how God sees you. Knowing yourself and who you are are the first obligations of a believer. Not knowing who you are means you are nothing, just a wisp of straw carried away by the wind. You exist, but only as a biological being, like an animal.

You must know your reputation, the perception that others have of you. You must also know your personality, at least, that part of your personality you, yourself, have built. You know your character well. You can fool others but not yourself. Think about what you do when no one is watching you; this will tell you a lot about your character.

If you are honest in your analysis, the image of yourself that you will discover will be less glorious than the narcissistic image you always had of yourself, but this image will be closer to the vision God has of you.

Listen to Your Inner Voice

God has put the Spirit in you. In the depths of your consciousness, he deposited the answers to the questions to yourself, says the Bible. "Counsel in the heart of man is like deep water; but a man of understanding will draw it out." (Prv 20:5)

It's your intuition that helps you make the right decision when the choice is not apparent. Intuition often suggests the answer, even before you had the time to think about the issue. The Bible says that you must "Be renewed in the spirit of your mind" (Eph 4:23), that is, you must always ask yourself questions and challenge your understanding of things, under the lighting of your continually renewed spirit.

Exploring your inner self involves digging deep into your

subconscious, a place well separated from your mindfulness, your state of awareness. In the unconscious, your life information dwells, a kind of life manual, which you have been endowed with at birth; what you need to do to survive, to protect your offspring, to multiply and take care of your family? What you need to do right after your birth, and many others. Usually, this information is available to you when the need arises, but the rest of the time, you must search for it. This safe contains invaluable treasures that you must take to the surface to enjoy. Yes, but how can one carry such a substantial wealth to the surface? You must dig into it, search and sort, and bring back to the surface what is useful to you. Then, you must deposit it in your conscience, your memory. When your inner voice calls you, it would be foolish to ignore it. The Bible says, "Let us search and try our ways, and turn again to the Lord." (Lam 3:40).

At birth, your soul was immaculate and sin-free, for God created you in his image. You were born holy, but then, slowly but inexorably, you went astray. This drift is not the result of a wrong decision. No one has ever said to himself in his early childhood: when I grow up, I'll be a thief or a liar. The Bible says: Sinners often say they believe they never committed sin, when in actual fact, they did. "Thou art of purer eyes than to behold evil, and canst not look on iniquity" (Hb 1:13) According to the famous saying, the road to hell is paved with good intentions.

How then could you do an honest self-examination if you are convinced beforehand that you are on the right path? The Bible says: "Every way of a man is right in his own eyes." (Prv 21:2) There are no such things as exhaustive lists of good and bad deeds. There are no pre-established models to imitate. That is why you must create a personal protective morality. You must get used to cherishing the right path. It is by seeking deep within yourself, where the divine light dwells, that you will find the answer. The

Apostle Paul said, "Know ye not that ye are the temple of God, and that the Spirit of God dwelleth in you?" (1 Cor 3:16). It is by questioning your own intuition, your inner voice, that you will learn who you are. Paul also says, "Let every man prove his own work" (Gal 6:4). The Scriptures speak of self-examination and self-evaluation helped by God. Like the psalmist, seek God's help and ask "Examine me, O Lord, and prove me; try my reins and my heart." (Ps 26:2).

You are the temple of God, and the Spirit of God dwells in you. It is by questioning your own intuition, your inner voice, that you will learn who you are. Your intuition is your safest guide if you know how to listen to your inner voice. Your intuition will make sure that you are on the right path. Interrogate your intuition as often as needed, and trust it.

C. Your Relationship with God

If you arrived at this paragraph, it means you have accomplished the hardest. You can be proud of yourself and of the work you have done. You have clarified and improved your relationships with others, and you now understand why it is so important to put the other before you in all circumstances, under the Golden Rule and the Royal Law. You comprehend why loving your neighbor ought to be at the foreground of your concerns. You are resolved and happy to be at the third rank, after God, and after your neighbor. The Bible says: "I have set the Lord always before me: because he is at my right hand, I shall not be moved." (Ps 16:8) You have eliminated many bad habits you had let grow over time, like seashells and algae that cling to the hulls of boats and prevent them from moving forward. You have regained control of your ego, and you have tamed your tongue. Finally, you got rid of some mistakes and vanities that weighed on your soul.

You have refocused your life. Now, you exist for the others more than for your own self, and you will enjoy with delight the new relationships you will have with your relatives, your friends, and with others. You know that they love you, and you know most of all that they rely on you and how much they need you. Your soul has been sublimated, and now it makes sense. You are no longer this selfish and lonely traveler, wandering aimlessly around his own belly button, capable of enjoying life, but inept at loving; Capable of existing but not of living; Capable of taking but inept at giving; Wishing to be loved but incapable of loving anyone.

Be proud of the new person you have become. The divine peace is in you. You are on the path of sanctification, and you can now develop an extraordinary relationship with God.

As with other types of relationships, the relationship with God involves three parties, of which you are the second; The third one being the divine Creation, and the first being the Lord. Interaction between all three parties to this relationship is required for a healthy relationship. If needed, read again Law # 2, God's Will, to be convinced of it.

You are his creature, and God is your Creator. Everything you need, only God can give it to you. You depend totally on him. It is illusory to think that you could manage your needs on your own. When God created the universe, the trees did not bear fruit, the plants did not carry seeds, for he had first to send rain, and he still had to create men. Once men were created, they had to till the soil and grow plants and vegetables to ensure their livelihood and that of their brethren and cattle. Plants needed water, so, men invoked God, and God sent rain on the earth. The Bible says: "In the day that the Lord God made the earth and the heavens, And every plant of the field before it was in the earth and every herb of the field before it grew: for the Lord God had not caused it to rain upon the earth, and there was not a man to till the ground" (Gn 2:4–5) When God heard man's supplication, he sent the rain, and the plants produced germs, and the fruit trees bore fruit, thanks to the gift of God and the work of man, nourishing greenery covered the earth. The Bible says: "The earth which drinketh in the rain that cometh oft upon it, and bringeth forth herbs meet for them by whom it is dressed, receiveth blessing from God" (Heb 6:7) This is how a lasting relationship is established between God and men; men invoke God and God gives them everything they need to fulfill His will.

The Heavenly Cord

You are familiar with your navel; this little hole in your abdomen also called the belly button. The navel is an abdominal scar that results from the removal of the newborn's umbilical cord. The umbilical cord is the link that connects the mother to the baby she carries. It contains two arteries and a vein through which all the exchanges occur, and it allows the mother to provide her baby with everything that he needs for his development: food, oxygen, thermal regulation, antibodies, waste disposal, Etc.

Just after birth, the physician cuts this cord, and the newborn becomes autonomous. He takes his first breath of fresh air that fills his lungs, as maternal oxygen is no longer available to him. As the newborn is no longer fed through the umbilical cord, he feels hunger a new and uncomfortable feeling. The baby understands that something has changed; he is not receiving food, and he is alarmed. He sends signals by screaming and trepidation of his whole body. He wants to tell everyone that he exists and that he needs immediate attention, that is, food and care.

As adults, they might want to learn one or more foreign languages, and they can do it, provided they put a lot of effort into it, for they will never regain their primal aptitudes. When they grow up and lose these exceptional aptitudes, it will become harder for them to learn another language. This is also your story, and even if you have no recollection of it, your navel is there to remind it to you.

In his early months, the newborn knows a rapid growth and particularly its brain. Billions of brain cells called neurons are created, and these neurons establish multiple communication channels between one another. Thanks to this vast network of synaptic connections, the newborn is exceptionally gifted. Newborns are apt to understand and learn all existing human languages, including those that are the most difficult to learn for adults. They could go and live in any foreign country, and they would meet no difficulty in acquiring the local language. But then, by a natural phenomenon that scientists call apoptosis, or programmed cell death, synaptic links and neurons not used, would self-destruct. Thus, in their development, the newborn's aptitude to learn any human language is washed out and other incredible talents.

What you may not know is there was also another cord, an immaterial cord that connected you to God. This heavenly cord is not cut off at birth, for it is not made of flesh. However, it gradually fades away, in a similar way that unused brain cells do, in what looks like spiritual apoptosis. You used that heavenly cord to communicate with God in your prenatal life and to receive from him whatever your nascent spirituality needed to prepare you to face life on earth. It is probably that same channel that God used to put his Spirit in your soul and to send you intuitions and inspiration.

Newborns are not only exceptionally gifted, multi-talented, and well fitted to face the challenges of life, but they are holy. Being without blemish, they are immaculate. They never sinned. They hurt no one. They never knew the temptation, and they never strayed far from the way of God. However, although they were born holy, they won't stay that way. Once their primal state of holiness has disappeared, so has their unique connection to God.

Should you feel the desire to become sanctified and to get closer to God, you will need to recreate this unique bond, the primal link that connected you to the Lord, that you had enjoyed before and immediately after birth. You can still learn a foreign language as an adult after you lost the exceptional aptitude to learn any foreign language, but you will have to work hard to succeed.

As soon as you can, you must endeavor to recreate a new close and personal connection to God.

Talking with God

Any relationship is based on communication, and the same is valid for relationships with God. Talk with God; even if he does not answer by voice, he always responds. A conversation with the Lord may be as simple as, "O Lord my God, help me," or "O Lord! Stand by me; I need you."

The Bible says: "With thee is the fountain of life: in thy light shall we see light." (Ps 36: 9) Talking with God is essential to establishing a healthy and lasting relationship with Him. Talk to him, and the inexhaustible riches of his grace will be there for you when you open up to him. Just as you speak with your friends to maintain your friendship, you must talk to God, open up to him with confidence, and be attentive to his answer, for the source of life is with him.

Trust the Lord! He loves you, and he will guide you, and he will stand by you in everyday life, through his Spirit of which he filled you with. The Bible says: "Trust in the Lord with all thine heart; and lean not unto thine own understanding. In all thy ways acknowledge him, and he shall direct thy paths." (Prv 3:5–6) Talk with God through sanctification and supplication.

Now that you master the essential biblical precepts for preparing yourself for sanctification, you can be proud of this accomplishment. You are well on your way to sanctification, and you are ready to undertake your most beautiful journey. At the end of the road, God is waiting for you. Don't give up!

Ignore them and bear the consequences

Law #4
The Law of Ends & Means

"Ye ask, and receive not, because ye ask amiss" (Jas 4:3)

You don't know how to ask

When Christ asked the sons of Zebedee, James, and John, "What would ye that I should do for you?" (Mk 10:35–45, Mt 20:20–23) the two brothers gave a bold answer: "Grant unto us that we may sit, one on thy right hand, and the other on thy left hand, in thy glory." (Mk 10:37) Christ was shocked at this excessive demand, and he replied: "Ye know not what ye ask." (Mt 20:22)

However, admit that this is in that same manner you ask, in the secret of your supplications. The Scripture says, "Ye ask, and receive not, because ye ask amiss." (Jas 4:3). Your requests lack humbleness, and they are only motivated by your selfish desire to receive and possess, regardless of the needs of others, and without consideration for your sacred duty to work towards fulfilling the Divine Will, in total contempt of the word of God.

In the verses quoted in the preceding paragraph, after the shocking demand of the sons of Zebedee, Christ taught them how to ask. Jesus said, "Can ye drink of the cup that I drink of?"

(Mk 10:38). Christ alludes to his own sacrifice and his death on the cross, which happened soon gives.

Asking is not an act done lightly. Asking is accomplished through a Supplication. It is an act of faith which implies a total commitment by the supplicant, like Christ, who offered himself to the ultimate sacrifice for the remission of our sins.

When you think you are making a Supplication, you are most likely making just a humble prayer that does not come from the bottom of your heart, but from a man-made prayer book. You don't know how you must ask, and you don't know how to supplicate. Through your pre-written prayers, you ask for anything and everything.

Some of your requests might be legitimate, while some others are not. For instance, asking for money or for winning the jackpot at the lottery is not justified; There are things you ought never to ask for, longer life for yourself or for a loved one for instance; Superfluous gifts like a quick weight loss, so you may put on clothes at your size ten years ago, for example.

I remember the story of a young relative who married a neighbor she had been secretly attracted to for years. She claimed that God had heard her prayers, for she had been praying God every day she would marry a man in all aspects like this gentleman.

She did marry him, but, just a few months into her newly found happiness, she found that her husband had been cheating on her since day one. Everyone around her seemed to know this man was a womanizer. She divorced and never remarried, for, in her prayers, she vowed that if the Lord answered her petitions, she would never have another man in her life.

So, what can you legitimately ask, and how should you ask for it? The answer is in the Bible.

How Should You Ask?

"Ask, and they will give you; Seek, and you will find; Knock, and they shall be opened unto you. (Mt 7:7, Lk 11:9) To ask, to seek, to knock, three degrees of progression that highlight the persistent and ever-increasing intensity, up to the climax. This biblical three-word approach, ask, seek, knock, is the most appropriate for those who seek to receive from God what they long for. Ask what you need and don't have; Seek for answers to what you don't know; Knock on doors to be admitted where you feel excluded. Repeat with insistence each of these three requirements, and be assured of the success of your efforts, says the Bible. "If we ask any thing according to his will, he heareth us" (1 Jn 5:14)

"Ask," suggests that you know having a material or spiritual deficiency, a lack of something that is essential to your life, although you have, deep inside you, the intuition you could obtain what you need.

"Seek," suggests that you wander like a lost soul, for you have lost contact with God, your guide. You have no one to guide you, and you no longer relate with the Lord, who alone can help you and fill the lack you feel in the depths of your being. The inner voice in your subconscious, where dwells the spirit that God has placed in you, alerts you and urges you to seek how you could repair this broken bond, and regain the benevolence and divine blessing.

"Knock," here means in plain language: knock on all doors until one opens to you; Listen to all sources, interrogate the nature around you; Try to understand what the divine will is and what God wants you to do. Do it with all the willpower you are capable of; Commit yourself fully, with diligence and perseverance. Leave no stone unturned. Knock and knock again at all doors, until finally, a door opens, and someone lets you come in and agree to answer your questions. To get closer to God and reconnect

Ignore them and bear the consequences

with him, you must open your way by yourself. Don't give up until you reach the purpose of your quest, restore your soul in his image, and until you may finally reconnect with him.

God gives to those who ask, provided that they ask what they may legitimately request and as they should ask. Whether they are rich and famous, or underprivileged and modest; healthy or in bad health; master or servant; well-educated or uneducated, God welcomes everyone, provided they are moved by true faith and humbleness. The Bible says: "All things, whatsoever ye shall ask in prayer, believing, ye shall receive." (Mt 21:22). The Scripture compares this with the attitude of parents and their willingness to give their children everything they ask for and even more. Parents are moved by a strong desire to please their children. However, God is wiser, and he knows much better what everyone needs. He knows what you desire, but above all, he knows what is right for you beyond your own desires.

The Bible says, "Your Father knoweth what things ye have need of, before ye ask him." (Mt 6:8).

A father or a mother will never deceive their child by giving him something harmful, just to avoid giving him what he wants. The Bible says: "If a son shall ask bread of any of you that is a father, will he give him a stone? or if he ask a fish, will he for a fish give him a serpent?" (Lk 11:11) So, how could we imagine that God could deceive someone or willfully commit a harmful act? How might anyone possibly think that the Heavenly Father could promise to give you what you asked him, but then gives you nothing, or worse, gives you something that will harm you?

When you invoke God, you must do it with absolute confidence, he will hear you. You must believe with all your soul he has given you what you ask him, or, better still, what he thinks best for you. How can you hope to be heard, if you doubt that God will listen to you? If you do not trust him, if your faith is not established, do not ask him! Do not make supplications! God will know that you are not sincere. He will know that your faith is faltering.

God knows better than the best parents what his children need. Even the best-intentioned parents don't have the wisdom God has. God does not always give what he was asked for, but he gives better because he knows what you need. He does not always give in the way you would like, but he provides in the way he deems most appropriate. God always keeps His promises.

The Bible says: "If we ask any thing according to his will, he heareth us." (1 Jn 5:14) The Scripture promises that everything you ask is given to you. Note it says "it is given to you" and not "will be given to you," for the Scripture also says, "If we know that he hear us, whatsoever we ask, we know that we have the petitions that we desired of him." (1 Jn 5:15); And: "What things soever ye desire, when ye pray, believe that ye receive them, and ye shall have them." (Mk 11:24). If, during your supplication, you have the slightest doubt that everything you ask is given to you, what is the point of wasting your time?

The Scripture says: "Let him ask in faith, nothing wavering." (Jas 1:6).

Be persistent in your queries. According to Seneca, the Roman philosopher, "He who asks timidly, teaches others to refuse." Christ taught to be persistent. The Scripture says, "He [Jesus] spake a parable unto them to this end, that men ought always to pray, and not to faint" (Lk 18:1).

Make supplications early in your life, for life is short, but eternal life is within your reach! If you do not act soon enough and with determination, how do you intend to justify the reason for your existence? What have you done with your life? And how are you going to explain your lack of action when comes the time to account?

If, during the Supplication, you have the slightest doubt

Ignore them and bear the consequences

that all the things you are asking are already given to you, don't continue. Why should you waste your time? If your faith is not firmly established or if doubt remains in you and you ask without belief, the conditions for a Supplication are not there.

Behold the Newborn

You know you must ask because asking is intuitive. Asking and receiving is evidence of an existing relationship. Those who ask, but don't obtain, don't have an established relationship with God. The first act of a newborn is to ask. When the newborn asks, he does not ask for a favor; he demands, in a very irreverent manner, immediate satisfaction of his needs—food, and care. Babies don't send their requests to someone in their entourage, in particular; They simply call upon the Providence. Babies are not specific about what they need, as they are not yet capable of evaluating their needs, but they are confident in their inner voice that says that God knows better than anybody else what their needs are right now. The Bible says: "Blessed is the man that trusteth in the Lord, and whose hope the Lord is." (Jer 17:7). Intuition tells them to ask high and loud, and with persistence, so that their requests are heard, and fulfilled with no delay. It is the spirit that God has placed in his heart that dictates to him to do so.

It is usual for the newborn child to demand that its requests be fulfilled without delay for several reasons: (A) The newborn only requires what is necessary for its survival and well-being; And (B) It only requests what it needs at the very time it asks for it. It asks nothing that would be useful to him at a later time; (C) It doesn't ask for superfluous things; (D) he may demand so forcefully, for he depends entirely on the divine Providence; (E) The apparent irreverence in his manner of asking is but seeming, for the newborn is immaculate, it still is in a state of angelic grace he is still holy. Therefore, none of its actions can be suspected of being tainted with vice, sin, or intent to harm. It cannot offend by demanding to be heard immediately, for the newborn is holier than all those surrounding him.

The same goes for wildlife. The Bible says "The young lions roar after their prey, and seek their meat from God.":(Ps 104:21) In bird breeding facilities, at feeding time, the piercing squeals of the newly hatched chicks asking the providence for their food are overwhelmingly noisy, and they convey so well the urgency of their requests, that the care staff can be affected with stress.

Behold newborns. Besides their holiness and their effective way of asking, they have so much to teach you. In the first few months of their existence, many people see them as mouths to feed, diapers to change, and sleepless nights to endure. They content themselves in being patient, waiting for them to grow up and become less annoying and funnier. Try, instead, to be humble and consider the newborn for what it is, an experienced master in supplication who could guide you through a successful Supplication.

As a self-conscious and autonomous adult, you have preserved the instinct to ask; however, you no longer know what you may ask for and how to ask for it, because your needs, whether real or perceived have become multiple and are much more complicated than the relatively simple needs of a newborn. You ought to go back to your early days and see how genuine and how blessed you were before you lost it all. You only had to ask once, and you received, as simple as that. You knew what to ask and how to ask for it. Then, you grew up and got an education, and you acquired knowledge, but you gave up a lot of your incredible primal skills and talents. By the time you became a grown-up, you have lost the most valuable gifts you had, your holiness, and your unique personal relationship with God.

Ignore them and bear the consequences

You want to change course, and you want to become the angel you used to be. But, given how hard it is for you, now, to set priorities, you ask for anything and everything, thinking that your chances of getting at least something will be higher. However, you are not heard.

Learning how to ask necessitates lots of effort, commitment, and high willpower; but not asking amounts to condemn oneself to a life of unfruitful frustrations and difficulties with no success in sight. Understand what you can ask for and limit your requests to what you may ask. Poorly formulated petitions are often unsuccessful, and tainted ones are not heard. Always keep this verse in mind. "Ye ask, and receive not, because ye ask amiss." (Jas 4:3) It is enough, however, to demonstrate humility and wisdom, in the first place, and to learn how to ask, says the Bible. "Teach us what we shall say unto him; for we cannot order our speech by reason of darkness [for we are too ignorant to address Him]." (Jb 37:19).

What Can You Ask?

Ask God "gifts that should be sought," says John Damascene, a medieval theologian also known as John of Damascus. John Damascene simply defines what to ask for and leaves it to you to decide whether the object of your request meets his definition. But what are these gifts that should be sought? Before asking, how can you ensure that your petition is legitimate and that it will be heard? The Scriptures are full of clues and advice.

Paul advises seeking above all non-material goods, "Seek those things which are above" (Col 3:1), that is, goods not of material nature. These goods from above are of divine origin. They are by nature intangible, so why ask for immaterial goods when you think you need money? The answer is simple: nobody needs money! If this statement surprises you or if you find it hard to believe, it is time for you to meditate about it, and hopefully, you'll be convinced. You may need things you usually buy with money; Food, clothing, housing, medicines, etc., but you do not need money. You can't eat money, for money is not food; You can't make clothes with banknotes; You can't build for yourself a house with coins and banknotes; Money cannot be used to heal your wounds or cure your illnesses. You may need food, clothing, shelter, medicine, etc., but you do not need money. So why ask for money, when you should ask for food, clothing, lodging, etc.?

Consider the purpose of your request carefully, without worrying about how it should be accomplished, for the means are God's privilege, exclusively. The Lord said, "My thoughts are not your thoughts, neither are your ways my ways." (Is 55: 8). You must admit once and for all nobody needs money! Money is not an end. Money is not a divine creation; it is man's invention. Money exists neither in the animal world, which is free from superfluity nor in God's work, which is also exempt from frivolities. When you think that you need money, you ought to immediately correct yourself and understand that you need something that you are accustomed to buying with cash. But money is so present in your mind you are persuaded that this is what you need and that you could not live without it. You confuse the ends with the means and money with divine providence. You create a golden idol comparable to the golden calf, and you worship it, you idolize it.

The Bible says: "Their idols are silver and gold, the work of men's hands." (Ps115: 4).

By asking for money, you make your request illegitimate. The Bible says: "Ye ask amiss" (Jas 4:3) Go back to square one, resume your Supplication at the very beginning. Your spirituality is in bad shape. By serving your idol, you will get trapped. The Bible says, "They served their idols: which were a snare unto them."

(Ps 106:36). And: "They that observe lying vanities forsake their own mercy." (Jon 2:8). Listen to the psalmist and restore your trust in God.

The Bible says, "I have hated them that regard lying vanities: but I trust in the Lord." (Ps 31:6).

Solomon's prayer is a unique teaching on how to design a Supplication that pleases God. When God appeared to Solomon and said to him, "Ask what I shall give thee." (2 Chr 1:7) Solomon answered (2 Chr 1:10). The Bible says, "And the speech pleased the Lord, that Solomon had asked this thing." (1 Kgs 3:10). And God said to Solomon, "because this was in thine heart, and thou hast not asked riches, wealth, or honour, nor the life of thine enemies, neither yet hast asked long life; but hast asked wisdom and knowledge for thyself, that thou mayest judge my people, over whom I have made thee king: Wisdom and knowledge is granted unto thee; and I will give thee riches, and wealth, and honour, such as none of the kings have had that have been before thee, neither shall there any after thee have the like." (2 Chr 1:11–12).

Does this mean it is permissible to ask only for intangible goods and to exclude anything material? Certainly not! There are material goods you can ask for, others that you ought to ask, and others that you would be wise not to ask.

The Scripture says, "Give us this day our daily bread." (Mt 6:11, Lk 11:3). This verse gives us two important clues: 1) It is permissible to ask for material goods if these goods are essential to your subsistence or to your survival. The bread symbolizes the vital foods, which excludes elaborate dishes that not only nourish but are also a source of pleasure, that of tasting and that of satisfaction for instance; 2) It is permissible and even recommended asking for what can satisfy an essential need at the very instant it is requested. Matthew's "this day" is, in this sense, superior to Luke's "day by day," for it means "the food we need to survive today." It is inappropriate to ask for goods you plan to amass for future use, for speculation, or to satisfy needs not yet born, but which may arise. Those who hoard things always do so to the detriment of others. If the products deteriorate or are lost, they can no longer be useful to anyone.

The Bible says, "Behold the fowls of the air: for they sow not, neither do they reap nor gather into barns; yet your heavenly Father feedeth them." (Mt 6:26).

Agur demonstrates his wisdom when he asks the Lord "Remove far from me vanity and lies: give me neither poverty nor riches; feed me with food convenient for me" (Prv 30:8). Paul wrote to Timothy, "And having food and raiment let us be shipment content." (1 Tm 6:8). When Jacob invoked the Lord, before undertaking a great journey, he contented himself with a vow "If God will be with me, and will keep me in this way that I go, and will give me bread to eat, and raiment to put on, So that I come again to my father's house in peace; then shall the Lord be my God" (Gn 28:20–21). Requests for material things must, preferably, be limited to those that meet essential needs.

The Bible says: "All things are lawful unto me, but all things are not expedient: all things are lawful for me, but I will not be brought under the power of any." (1 Cor 6:12) In a petition, you ought to strive to ask for what you need at this very moment, and only what you need at that moment. God, should he hear you, will only grant you what you need, not what you would have liked to receive. You could well get more than what you requested, for you had no means to know the full extent of your needs.

Agur's Supplication

Agur's supplication to God sounded like the last wishes of a man who longed to leave to his descendants the legacy

Ignore them and bear the consequences

of the wisdom that had so profoundly marked his life. In his supplication, Agur limited his requests to two things. The first is a most precious thing, which God grants to all who ask for it with enthusiasm, and which he had once given to Solomon, who had asked for "wisdom and knowledge." Agur asked God to be preserved from falsehood. "Remove far from me vanity and lies" (Prv 30:8a) Then, Agur formulated another request, he asked for what he considered necessary for living with dignity "give me neither poverty nor riches" (Prv 30: 8b). The Lord is not likely to frequently receive petitions, where the petitioner is adamant about his not wanting to obtain wealth. The opposite is accurate, usually. Fortunately, Agur also expressed his desire not to be afflicted by poverty; otherwise, some might have thought he was out of his mind. Why was Agur not interested in wealth? Most people would never think of asking God not to give them wealth. Was Agur so different from others? The answer is yes! Agur was wise, far wiser than the average person. Agur believed in the promise of the Scripture. The Scripture says, "My God shall supply all your need" (Phil 4:19). Why should Agur be interested in amassing wealth, when all that he needed was to be assured he would receive his daily bread? In his sermon on the mountain, Christ said "Lay not up for yourselves treasures upon earth, where moth and rust doth corrupt, and where thieves break through and steal"(Mt 6:19). Likewise, in his supplication, Agur asked "feed me with food convenient for me" (Prv 30:8c). Isn't this what Christ taught later in his sermon on the mountain, in his prayer to the Father? Christ knew well the verses of the Old Testament, and he had probable he had been inspired by Agur's supplication, Christ said. "Give us this day our daily bread." (Mt 6:11) Agur asked the Lord only for the minimum he needed for his subsistence. Everything else was for him superfluous.

Wise men know well their own weaknesses and their limits,

and they know those of men in general. They know that extreme poverty can lead the afflicted to the temptation of stealing to provide for their essential needs. Agur wanted to depend solely on the divine providence for all his needs. He knew that wealth could take him away from God, for material goods, when they are too abundant, require that someone look after them full time, and this precious time which ought to have been devoted to God will be spent for guarding superfluous goods.

The modesty and humility Agur demonstrated in his requests are a lesson to remember. Agur knew that men belong to one of two groups: those who love to give, and those who never tire of receiving. Agur said, "The horseleach hath two daughters, crying, Give, give." (Prv 30:15).

Solomon's Supplication

Solomon is the author of one of the most remarkable supplications, a supplication that pleased the Lord so much that God heard it, and he granted Solomon much more than what he had asked for. Solomon had asked, "Give me now wisdom and knowledge" (2 Chr 1:10). And God said to Solomon "Because this was in thine heart, and thou hast not asked riches, wealth, or honour, nor the life of thine enemies, neither yet hast asked long life; but hast asked wisdom and knowledge for thyself, that thou mayest judge my people, over whom I have made thee king: Wisdom and knowledge is granted unto thee; and I will give thee riches, and wealth, and honour, such as none of the kings have had that have been before thee, neither shall there any after thee have the like." (2 Chr 1:11–12). Solomon asked for wisdom, and he justifies why. "The Lord giveth wisdom: out of his mouth cometh knowledge and understanding." (Prv 2: 6).

Ignore them and bear the consequences

Hezekiah's Supplication

Hezekiah became king at twenty-five, and he reigned twenty-nine years over Jerusalem and the kingdom of Judah. The account of his reign is told in the Bible, in 2 Kgs 18–20, Is 36–39, and 2 Chr 29–32. Hezekiah is remembered as a righteous and enlightened king. During the siege of Jerusalem by the Assyrian armies, Hezekiah had fallen gravely ill. As he was lying down on his bed, he was visited by Isaiah, the prophet whom God had sent to his bedside to tell him that his time on earth was about to expire and that he should think of putting his affairs in order, to facilitate his succession. Hezekiah knew that if he died, his people could not protect themselves from Assyrians. The Bible tells the story of the miraculous remission from his severe illness that may well have been terminal cancer. What happened afterward ought to be meditated and remembered. The Bible says that after he had received God's announcement, Hezekiah turned his face against the wall, and simply supplicated to the Lord. "I beseech thee, O Lord, remember now how I have walked before thee in truth and with a perfect heart, and have done that which is good in thy sight." (2 Kgs 20:3) Isaiah had gone out, but he had not exited the property yet when the Lord ordered him to return to Hezekiah's bedside and inform him of his new decision, "I have heard thy prayer, I have seen thy tears: behold, I will heal thee: on the third day thou shalt go up unto the house of the Lord. And I will add unto thy days fifteen years; and I will deliver thee and this city." (2 Kgs 20:5–6). Fifteen years later, Hezekiah died, as God had willed.

Why Is this Supplication So Noteworthy?

This supplication is a remarkable illustration of what an effective Supplication should be. Hezekiah, who had been pious throughout his life, would not fall into the traps in which a less devout man, less trained in speaking with the Lord, could have fallen. Hezekiah's supplication was spontaneous. He did not elaborate and did not ask for something specific. He did not ask God to heal him, nor did he ask him to extend his life. Hezekiah relied entirely on God's will. He simply reminded him he had always lived according to his will. Yes, would you say, but he has not pleaded to benefit the highest number! Wrong! When he made this supplication, the kingdom of Hezekiah had been partly occupied by the Assyrians to launch the final assault to take Jerusalem. Without their leader, his people would have suffered. Jerusalem would have been captured and plundered, and his people would have been massacred or enslaved. Hezekiah knew well that he did not need to recall all these facts to the Lord. Everything he could express by words was sublimated in his short prayer. All his requests and his distress are conveyed by this petition otherwise meager in words, although more effective than a long speech. The response of the Lord was immediate. God told him that he would A) heal him of his illness; B) extend his life by fifteen more years; C) protect Jerusalem from the Assyrians; D) and protect the people of Jerusalem.

This is what happened. The Assyrians were struck with a scourge that the Lord had sent to them (Is 37:36, 2 Chr 32:21), which decimated one hundred and eighty-five thousand Assyrian soldiers in one night. The Bible says: "Sennacherib king of Assyria departed, and went and returned, and dwelt at Nineveh." (2 Kgs 19:36) In Nineveh, Sennacherib, king of Assyria, was murdered by his own children.

Ignore them and bear the consequences

What Did Hezekiah Receive?

1. What could have happened had Hezekiah simply asked to be healed of his illness? Well, once healed, he might have had to go to war against the Assyrian army, with the possibility of either winning or losing, knowing he would not have received God's help in the scourge that decimated the Assyrian army. Plus, Sennacherib could have raised fresh troops and launched a new offensive, had he not, meanwhile, been murdered by his own children.

2. What would have happened if Hezekiah had only asked for a longer life? Answer: he could have lived fifteen years longer, but ill and weakened by the disease; He might have lost the battle against the king of Assyria, who could have made him prisoner. He could have been sent at Nineveh into slavery, with the other exiled survivors of Jerusalem, and there he might have had a life far longer than he had asked for, only to die after fifteen years of suffering.

Now, you understand why Hezekiah's supplication was perfect. In a Supplication, the scarcity of words is often superior to a long speech. In relying entirely on the will of the Lord, Hezekiah had been well inspired by his intuition. The long-lasting relationship that Hezekiah had entertained with the Lord dispensed him of having to make elaborate speeches to be heard. It was sufficient for him to remind God he had always observed his commandments. Additional words, therefore, became superfluous.

3. Why did God extend Hezekiah's life by fifteen years, when one or two years would have been a remission of his illness long enough to win the war? Don't forget that God had also promised Hezekiah that he would protect Jerusalem from the Assyrians, and significant works would be needed to protect the city, before, during, and after the siege.

4. What did Hezekiah do after his miraculous healing and the

fifteen long extra years of life that God had given him generously? Hezekiah consolidated the defenses of his capital, Jerusalem. He constructed a dam upstream of the Gihon River and diverted its waters to the city of Jerusalem by a tunnel dug in the rock (2 Kgs 20:20; 2 Chr 32:30). Within the city walls, he dug a large reservoir, according to the Bible. "Hezekiah prospered in all his works." (2 Chr 32:30).

5. Why had Hezekiah been so quickly and so exhaustively answered? You might think that if such a short supplication had been enough for Hezekiah to obtain such fantastic results, why not you? Well, good reasoning! In the same circumstances, you might probably get the same results. However, are the conditions identical? When Hezekiah made his supplication, he had been sanctified "Whatsoever we ask, we receive of him, because we keep his commandments, and do those things that are pleasing in his sight." (1 Jn 3:22).

Hezekiah had established a strong personal relationship with the Lord. Since long ago, he had accomplished the long journey you will just begin. But you are on the right track. Your journey will be much less trying for you, for you won't have to fight against the mighty armies of Assyria, and you won't have to divert rivers nor consolidate the fortifications of your city. However, you must face an even more formidable enemy: yourself, your ego, the corrupt version of your person, before you become or rather, before you become once again, holy as you were at birth.

What did Socrates Say?

Socrates, the Greek philosopher of antiquity, was of the opinion we ought to ask God for nothing else than "What God thinks he should give us," for the Lord knows what everyone needs. Whereas, too often in our supplications, we ask, in good

Ignore them and bear the consequences

faith or by ignorance, things we should not request, for instance, money, unnecessary material goods, and other vanities like honors and distinctions, that generate corruption and iniquities.

His reasoning is relevant in terms of logic; however, he does not consider an essential factor: the effort of reflection and introspection that leads the supplicant to carefully choose what the object of his supplication ought to be, and how he should request it. This spiritual approach is an integral and inalienable part of the process of Supplication, and cannot be ignored in any circumstances.

Everything you ask, God alone can give it to you. If the Lord sees fit to satisfy your requests, it is to ensure that his will is accomplished. It is therefore useless to ask that which do not participate, directly or indirectly, in fulfilling his will, since his designs are superior and nothing is more important than their accomplishment.

What Did the Apostles Say?

John thought we should ask what God wants, and according to his will. The Scripture says, "If we ask any thing according to his will, he heareth us" (1 Jn 5:14).

Paul says that in our requests, we should include spiritual goods before all. The Scripture says, "Seek those things which are above" (Col 3:1). However, Paul also teaches that prayers and supplications should not be selfish acts, and must be done to benefit all mankind. The Scripture says, "I exhort therefore, that, first of all, supplications, prayers, intercessions, and giving of thanks, be made for all men." (1 Tm 2:1).

James also considered wisdom as an essential good. The Scripture says, "If any of you lack wisdom, let him ask of God, that giveth to all men liberally, and upbraideth not; and it shall be given him." (Jas 1:5).

Zechariah advised asking for rain, for it makes grass and plants grow, which provides food for men and animals. What a beautiful example of wisdom and farsightedness! When God sends the rain, he answers the requirements of all living creatures; therefore, the selfless quality of an excellent Supplication is met. For Zechariah, it is useless to ask for anything but rain, for rain covers the entire earth with a carpet of nourishing verdure. The Bible says: "Ask ye of the Lord rain in the time of the latter rain; so, the Lord shall make bright clouds, and give them showers of rain, to every one grass in the field." (Zec 10:1) Do you realize that by asking only for rain, you and many others could receive everything you need? Do you understand why you will never need to ask for money?

Moses said the best gift of heaven is dew. Shortly before his death, Moses addressed his blessings to the children of Israel. "And of Joseph he said, blessed of the Lord be his land, for the precious things of heaven, for the dew..." (Dt 33:13).

We ought to ask God for nothing else than "What God thinks he should give us," for the Lord knows what everyone needs. Whereas, too often in our supplications, we ask, in good faith or by ignorance, things we should not request, for instance, money, unnecessary material goods, and other vanities like honors and distinctions, that generate corruption and iniquities. (Socrates)

What Did Christ Say?

Christ says that we should ask for gifts that other people are also asking for or gifts that will benefit the higher number of men, for God answers, first, to the requests that help the most considerable amount of people and to those that facilitate the fulfillment of His Will, according to the Scripture. "Again I say unto you, that if two of you shall agree on earth as touching anything that they shall ask, it shall be done for them of my Father which is in heaven." (Mt 18:19).

Christ himself had recourse to supplications, the Scripture says "in the days of his flesh, when he had offered up prayers and supplications with strong crying and tears unto him that was able to save him from death" (Heb 5:7). What is more human than not wanting to die? Every living creature, man or animal, possesses natural reflexes to defend themselves against death. When threatened with it, some animals flee because they have confidence in the strength and velocity of their limbs; Others prefer to face a threat and fight, for they trust the superiority of their fangs. Christ's power was in the Father; he believed in him and relied entirely on His Will. In the garden of Gethsemane, Christ invoked the Father and asked if he would remove the cup from him, the painful ordeal of the death on the cross. The Bible says: "Father, if thou be willing, remove this cup from me" (Lk 22:42a) Then, he hastened to add: "Not my will, but thine, be done." (Lk 22: 42b) Christ had thus expressed his desire that, although he had supplicated to ask the Father to remove from him the suffering and horrible death ahead of him, he clearly wanted, above all, that God responds according to his own Divine Will, and not to his personal request. This was a supreme act of faith, knowing this deliberate choice would lead him to die on the cross in horrible sufferings.

Christ taught his disciples to ask for protection from temptation. The Scripture says, "Pray that ye enter not into temptation." (Lk 22:40b).

Christ supplicated for the benefit of others besides himself.

The Scripture says, "Father, forgive them; for they know not what they do." (Lk 23:34b).

Christ always prayed, says the Bible. "He departed into a mountain to pray." (Mk 6:46b) And, "He withdrew himself into the wilderness, and prayed." (Lk 5:16).

Christ invoked God in supplication and asked for wisdom when he would choose his twelve apostles. The Scripture says, "He went out into a mountain to pray, and continued all night in prayer to God. And when it was day, he called unto him his disciples: and of them he chose twelve, whom also he named apostles." (Lk 6:12–13).

Greatest Supplications of the Bible

Agur's Supplication

"Remove far from me vanity and lies: give me neither poverty nor riches; feed me with food convenient for me." (Prv 30:8)

Solomon's Supplication

"Give me now wisdom and knowledge, that I may go out and come in before this people: for who can judge this thy people, that is so great?" (2 Chr 1:10).

Hezekiah's Supplication

"I beseech thee, O Lord, remember now how I have walked before thee in truth and with a perfect heart, and have done that which is good in thy sight. And Hezekiah wept sore." (2 Kgs 20: 3).

Ignore them and bear the consequences

Christ's Supplication

"Not my will, but thine, be done." (Lk 22:42b).

What Should You Not Ask?

Solomon's supplication and God's response to his requests teach what you should not ask: riches, material goods, glory, the death of your enemy, or a longer life, for all these things are divine privileges. Even requests that appear legitimate are sometimes not heard, for they do not have divine approval. At the request of the sons of Zebedee's mother, Christ answered "Ye know not what ye ask." (Mt 20:22) And he said "to sit on my right hand, and on my left, is not mine to give, but it shall be given to them for whom it is prepared of my Father." (Mt 20:23b).

Some things fall within God's reserved domain, and him alone, in his sole discretion, may decide whether to grant them or not. If the Lord gives them, they are justified; otherwise, they might create inequities and injustices. As the psalmist says, it is not permissible to ask what can generate unfairness. The Scripture says, "If I regard iniquity in my heart, the Lord will not hear me." (Ps 66:18). Why derogate for he who asks, at the risk of creating an injustice? Enriching he who requests does not participate in fulfilling the Divine Will. The purpose of these extra years of life, not from the divine will, but from your own, and therefore empty from God's purpose, what is their impact on fulfilling the Divine Will? The desire to live longer is only an egotistical desire that does not participate in fulfilling the divine will. God alone may decide the duration of the life of each one, and it is, therefore, useless to ask for a derogation. Nothing will do.

God's Privileges

Most fresh goods you buy at the supermarket come with an expiration date. The same goes for man. When God gives the gift of life, it comes with an expiration date. Unlike consumer goods, this date is not written anywhere, because God alone knows it.

With the divine blessings (gifts, graces), our expiration date, which means the time of our death, is one thing that belongs to God's exclusive domain. The same applies to the life length he has assigned to each of his creatures. These hidden things, he doesn't want us to know about them, and it would be futile to comprehend, influence, or modify them.

No one can have control over the date of his own death to postpone it to a later date. Hidden things, such as the time of the passing of a person, are not accessible to humans. All men know that such a day will come, but none knows when that will be. God willed it so. It is, therefore, not permissible to ask for hidden things. The Bible says: "The secret things belong unto the Lord our God" (Dt 29:29)

No one can extend the life of a loved one, even by prayers or supplications; and he who asks for the death of an enemy will not be heard. Those who do it are adepts of superstition, black magic, or any other form of witchcraft. Abstain from asking for those things which belong to God's exclusive domain, for God alone has the privilege to decide what he wants to do with them, with no influence.

Whether your requests will be heard or not; where, when, and how you will receive what you requested, also belongs to the domain of hidden things. Heaven has wisely hidden those things from human knowledge. No man knows it; not the wisest, not the most gifted. This is one secret thing which belongs to the Lord our God. No one can be more imaginative and subtle in this field. The lord's ways are impenetrable, it is said, but one might add that

Ignore them and bear the consequences

they are also surprising and unexpected. It is therefore unwise to negotiate how and when the delivery should be expected or the nature of the shipment. It is also not recommended to add in fine print that you would prefer a short-term cash settlement and small denomination banknotes.

The Bible says: "I waited patiently for the Lord; and he inclined unto me, and heard my cry." (Ps40:1) David had always hoped that God would hear him, and he had no doubt that he would be given; however, David also knew that he had to be patient. God acts as he wishes, and his gifts are delivered as and when he wants, for his ways are his ways. The LORD said, "My thoughts are not your thoughts, neither are your ways my ways." (Is 55:8).

God has expressed himself on the succession of acts and interventions that constitute his ways. The Scripture says, "And it shall come to pass in that day, I will hear, saith the Lord, I will hear the heavens, and they shall hear the earth; And the earth shall hear the corn, and the wine, and the oil; and they shall hear Jezreel." (Hos 2:21–22). On that day means, At the date of my choosing, I will hear the heavens, are an indication of the complexity of the divine ways, for God rarely responds to a person by direct means. God uses all the resources of the creation to respond to a request. By doing so, he tells us that all living things are connected and dependent on one another, and, together, they work at fulfilling God's will. Therefore, what one of them does affects the rest of them, and the whole creation benefits from it. Thus, when God hears the heavens and pours the rain, his whole Creation is activated, and his Will can be accomplished, and this is how his gifts finally reach the supplicant. In their turn, the heavens will hear the earth thirsty for rain. Once watered, the earth will hear the crops and help them produce cereals, vegetables, fruits, oil, and grass for the beasts. These agricultural productions, in their turn, will fulfill the needs of the people of Jezreel, a fertile valley of southern Galilee, in Israel, whose people had called upon the Lord to bless their harvests. Their petitions have been heard, their requests have been fulfilled, and now, they may enjoy prosperity. Isn't that a good demonstration of how the ways of the Lord and how the divine will work?

What Should you Absolutely Ask?

A) Forgiveness of sins

When you confess your sins, the Lord sees what was wrong in your life, and he helps you and provides you with everything you need to change. When you repent for your sins, he forgives you and gives you the strength to start anew on the right track.

David's life seemed regular, but his inner life was anchored on a fragile foundation. David had committed adultery and murder, and he had tried to keep his disloyal conduct secret. After Nathan had confronted him, on the very day of the birth of his son, born of his adulterous union with Bathsheba, David understood that denying sin would weaken the foundation of his spiritual life forever. To prevent his spiritual abyss from worsening, David, followed Nathan's advice and acknowledged his sin before God, with repentance.

The Bible says, "I acknowledge my sin unto thee, and mine iniquity have I not hid. I said, I will confess my transgressions unto the Lord; and thou forgavest the iniquity of my sin." (Ps 32:5)

God forgave him. However, God forgives, but he doesn't erase the sin nor its consequences. The Bible says: "The thing that David had done displeased the Lord." (2 Sm 11:27) And the child of sin would never enter into the covenant and would never be named, for the newborn was traditionally named after entering into the covenant through circumcision, on the eighth day "it came to pass on the seventh day, that the child died." (2 Sm 12:18)

B) Spirit, Intelligence and Wisdom

The Divine Spirit has left an imprint on all creatures. All have received, to varying degrees, spirit, intelligence, and wisdom, the fundamental organizing principles of the universe, which enable them to manage the relationships among themselves and their relationship with God and the Divine Creation.

Plants know they must turn towards the sun and expose itself to sunlight to capture its rays with the power to transform the chlorophyll that their leaves contain into energy, a phenomenon called photosynthesis. The thirsty earth knows it must ask the sky for rain. The wildlife knows what they must do to feed, protect, and take care of their offspring. The Bible says: "Wilt thou hunt the prey for the lion? or fill the appetite of the young lions" (Jb 38:39) And "Who provideth for the raven his food? when his young ones cry unto God, they wander for lack of meat." (Jb 38:41)

The Lord gives wisdom and intelligence to those who ask for it, for they are essential qualities for anyone who wants to work towards fulfilling His Will. The Book of Proverbs, the Book of Job, and the Ecclesiastes, are almost entirely devoted to wisdom. You ought to always ask for wisdom. The Bible says: "The Lord giveth wisdom: out of his mouth cometh knowledge and understanding." (Prv 2:6) As for James, "If any of you lack wisdom, let him ask of God, that giveth to all men liberally, and upbraideth not; and it shall be given him." (Jas 1:5). The Scripture says, "God giveth to a man that is good in his sight wisdom, and knowledge, and joy" (Eccl 2:26) And the Scripture also says, "Who hath put wisdom in the inward parts? or who hath given understanding to the heart?" (Jb 38:36)

Elihu, the intelligent young man, son of Barachel the Buzite, argued with Job and his friend Ram, explaining why he had felt he rightfully intervened in a discussion between elders, without waiting for them to exhaust their arguments, as decency demanded. He told them that although God had given wisdom to older men, he provided men of all ages with spirit and intelligence. Therefore, he was not un-respectful in participating in a debate between elders.

God gives intelligence, and it is, therefore, to him, we must ask for it. The Scripture says: "But there is a spirit in man: and the inspiration of the Almighty giveth them understanding." (Jb 32:8). This is what the psalmist and other biblical authors do. The Scripture says, "Behold, thou desirest truth in the inward parts: and in the hidden part thou shalt make me to know wisdom." (Ps 51:6) "Only the LORD grants you wisdom and understanding" (1 Chr 22:12)"As for these four children, God gave them knowledge and skill in all learning and wisdom: and Daniel had understanding in all visions and dreams." (Dn 1:17) "Yea, if thou criest after knowledge, and liftest up thy voice for understanding" (Prv 2:3)

Wisdom is the intelligence that God has given to the mind of man, enhanced and perfected by the imprint of time and the years of experience and by an ardent spirituality. God loves those who seek wisdom and understanding and who use them in their prayers. The Scripture says, "I will pray with the spirit, and I will pray with the understanding also." (1 Cor 14:15).

You always have the choice to act, whether wisely or according to your temptations. But, on the day of judgment, you will be nothing more or less than the sum of all your choices.

C) What Will Benefit the Greatest Number

Supplication is not a selfish or egocentric act. Even in the solitude of your approach, the other is always present. Ask for gifts and favors that will benefit the most significant number. If you, alone, make a supplication, God will hear it as coming from many persons if you associate others collectively, to receive the benefits of your Supplication.

The chances of being listened to are more significant when several people ask for the same thing, or when the asking person does not ask for his sole benefit, but to benefit a higher number. Christ said, "Again I say unto you, that if two of you shall agree on earth as touching anything that they shall ask, it shall be done for them of my Father which is in heaven." (Mt 18:19)

Don't ask, preferably, what may benefit you, and only you. How can we imagine that God can send rain to only one person who asked for it?

If the Lord wants to give rain, he will probably give it to all the victims of a drought in a region, for instance. If, however, more than one person made the same request, or if only one person has asked for rain for all those who suffer from the same drought, their petition will be granted.

To Be or Not to Be Heard?

Divine responses to petitions are of several kinds. Requests can simply be ignored, momentarily, or definitely; They can be partially or answered; The supplicant may also be granted gifts different from those he had requested; The supplicant may sometimes receive much more than just what he had wished, as for Solomon. The Bible says, "And I have also given thee that which thou hast not asked, both riches, and honour" (1 Kgs 3:13a) The divine response to certain supplications may contain a warning, with or without consequences. But in all cases, the Lord answers all Supplications, whether the supplicant acknowledges it or not.

Each answer is unique and sometimes contains a personal

message that God addresses to the supplicant. So, when you think that your petition has not been heard, this may be a sign you could have done better; that your request was ill-conceived or that it contained elements that you'd better have omitted. It could also mean that it contained something wrong or that you do not deserve to be answered. Finally, God may even ignore a legitimate petition for reasons that he alone knows.

A supplication ignored can always be renewed again and again indefinitely, but to have a better chance of being heard, you will need to improve it and show you have made a sincere and commendable effort to amend it or to remedy mistakes that might have rendered your request Illegitimate.

I have a childhood memory that I am not ready to forget. I was 8 or 10 years old. My neighbor was well known for her lottery addiction. Every week, she used a substantial part of her husband's retirement pension, to buy lottery tickets. She was convinced that, sooner or later, she would hit the jackpot. She had made plans for a future life of ease and freedom from want. She told everyone about her large-scale charitable projects because generosity was her only motivation. Although, to a close friend, she confessed another, less glorious, motivation, her desire of parting from her husband whose health was deteriorating day after day, for she did not want to spend the rest of her days caring for an infirm. She knew that one day, luck would smile at her, thanks to a secret prayer cut out from an old magazine that she recited three times a day with eagerness.

I remember that day when our little community was made aware that someone among them had won the jackpot, and they all went wild as if struck by lightning. A very kind and always smiling old man who lived in a small shed on the ground floor was the winner. He had never bought a lottery ticket in his entire life. The winning ticket had been offered to him two or three

Ignore them and bear the consequences

days earlier, for his birthday, by the nurses of the hospital where he had just undergone the amputation of a leg. He died a few weeks later of infection. When he received the payoff, he donated the whole sum to a community medical nursing foundation, so they could grant scholarships to needy nursing students. The neighbor's prayers had been answered, but so it was highly ethical and divine.

The gifts most frequently requested are often those that are not likely to be granted; Wealth, for example. Many people are convinced that wealth can bring them everything they need and solve all their problems.

It is a grave error of judgment because money has no real value. It's only worth the difference between the temporary joy it can bring and the lasting misfortunes they can engender. The stories of people who lead a healthy life, with a dose of small problems like everyone, and who, one day, made a fortune at the lottery, are well known. Some of these "winners" may have believed they had been freed forever of all their problems. Later, they bitterly regretted that they had won the jackpot, for the misfortunes that followed were far from being worth it. Money brings hope, but it also brings misfortune, says the Bible. "If we ask any thing according to his will, he heareth us" (1 Jn 5:14)

The petitions granted, totally or partially, and those that are fulfilled beyond what had been requested, are a truly divine blessing for the supplicant, for whom divine generosity is the proof that a dialogue has been established with God. He who receives the gift or grace of God is sanctified. His efforts to come closer to the Lord and to understand the Divine Will are rewarded.

But those who receive in response to their petition something that looks like a divine punishment should consider that it might be time for them to rethink in depth their spirituality and their way of life, even if they know that it might be too late to escape the consequences of their acts.

God forgives and does not punish sinners, but he doesn't forget, nor does he avert the consequences of their sins. Their supplications could have generated adverse effects, and they will bear the costs of their acts. It would be foolish for them to continue along the same path. The message is clear, they must find what has angered the Lord, and they must remedy it without delay.

Summary

- Ask what you may ask in a supplication.

- First, ask non-material goods like wisdom, joy, happiness, compassion, the ability to understand, ask the Lord to guide you in your decisions, Etc. These intangible goods elevate your soul and bring you closer to God.

- Among the material goods you can ask, those that are essential to your survival and dignity come to the fore: bread, water, a daily meal, a dwelling, and what you need to clothe yourself.

- Ask nothing that is superficial, vain, or excessive, or that exceeds your necessary and sufficient needs.

- Do not ask what has for sole purpose to please you, to satisfy your passions, or to satisfy your guilty desires to have what others have and which you do not have.

- Exclude from your petitions all that can create an injustice, favoring you to the detriment of others.

Ignore them and bear the consequences

- Don't trespass on God's prerogatives by asking for things that belong to his privileged domain, for instance, longer life for yourself or for someone else.

- Ask in priority what will also benefit others than you.

- Ask what is likely to be beneficial to the most significant number of people, and if need be, make your petition on behalf of many persons, even if it is understood that you will also benefit from the divine gifts, by the fact that you belong in the community of potential beneficiaries.

- Finally, ask what contributes, above all, to fulfilling the Divine Will.

Know, however, that the Lord will not feed you with a silver spoon; He is not your servant. God will give you everything you need to make a delicious meal, but you must add your own contribution to it, your sweat. If the Lord gives you a fertile land and sends abundant rain on this earth, you must roll up your sleeves and cultivate this land; otherwise, it will only produce grass. The LORD said, "In the sweat of thy face shalt thou eat bread" (Gn 3:19). When you harvest the fruit of your partnership with the Lord, you'll understand that many other creatures also brought their own skills to further your collaboration with the Lord. Think of the bees that pollinated the plants, the earthworms that brought oxygen and rainwater to the roots of your crops, for instance, and also think of the myriads of other tiny loyal partners like insects and bacteria that worked tirelessly in this broad partnership with the Lord, ultimately to benefit each one. And, with you, they will share the fruit of your association.

Humbleness is of the essence of a Supplication. Be humble, behold the newborns and take them for what they are, masters of Supplication who could teach you so much about the art of Supplication.

Newborns demand what they need, not what they desire, for they have no desires and no envy. Since their umbilical cord was severed, they have needs they cannot satisfy by themselves. But although you have fewer requirements, you have more longings. Your supplications are tarnished with unnecessary wants and envy, although you believe that you focus on your needs.

Newborns demand that their needs be fulfilled right away for they are still holy, but you are no more. Your endeavor in seeking sanctification will put you on the right track to recover at least some of your lost holiness.

Newborns only ask for what they need for their survival and well-being, and they only request what they need at the very time they ask for it. They ask nothing that would be useful to them at a later time. Newborns never ask for unessential things. They put all their confidence in the Divine Providence, and they know, without the shadow of a doubt, that God has already given them what they are just asking.

Remember that if you do not get what you request, it may be because God loves you.

Law #5
The Law of Gratitude

"Delight thyself also in the Lord: and he shall give thee the desires of thine heart." (Ps 37:4)

The Power of Alleluia

"Alleluia" is usually translated as "Praise the Lord!" This word that comes from the Hebrew "Hallelujah" comprises "Hallel" (praise), and "Yah," a contracted form of "Yahweh," the Lord. However, the translation "Praise the Lord," although it is technically correct, only partially renders the Hebrew word "Alleluia," which contains much more meaning than this translation reveals, for instance, that it also implies there can be no limit to the happiness of those who cry this word to God.

"Alleluia" is a short but important word, because it binds in a single word, not only the name of God and his glorification but also the act of adoration of the believer. Rendering this word in its fulness necessitates contemplating a third and even a fourth dimension to its translation, which would be vocal for one and emotional for the other. In the Bible, when the word "Alleluia" is pronounced, it is never softly. "Alleluia" is an exuberant clamor, an expression of extreme joy and happiness, a burst of joyfulness, a firework that illuminates the sky and fills all hearts with joy and happiness.

In the Scriptures, invocations and supplications are often called a cry to God, a strong appeal, not because God is far from us, and we need to raise our voice to get to be heard, but because a cry expresses a deep and urgent need. The supplicant cries to the Lord, as the baby calls upon the Divine Providence for his immediate needs to be satisfied. The Bible says, "Who provideth for the raven his food? when his young ones cry unto God" (Jb 38:41) And, "He [the Lord] giveth to the beast his food, and to the young ravens which cry." (Ps147:9).

It is a cry of the same nature you should use to implore God when you beg him to satisfy your needs, to console your afflictions, and to relieve your sufferings; and it is by this same cry you glorify the Lord. What a strange coincidence! But is this a coincidence? I don't think so. I think, on the contrary, that alleluia is one of the most beautiful words of the liturgical vocabulary, for it constitutes a profession of faith, an act of worship, praise and thanksgiving, and that it is essential to anyone who wants to supplicate to God and to create a strong relationship with him. I simply regret that although it is still considered today as a consecrated interjection, much of its meaning and strength have been lost in translations. "Praise the Lord!" does not have the same resonance as a resounding "alleluia" gushing from a thousand fervent hearts.

How to understand the spiritual power of an alleluia cried simultaneously by the voice of many fervent believers? How can one feel the effect produced by this simple word? Imagine for a moment you are an athlete. You are participating in a significant competition. You have no illusions about your chances of getting on the podium, as you compete against more experienced athletes. In the crowd of spectators, your relatives and friends are there to cheer you. But an inner voice tells you you are there to win and that you must not give up just because you believe others are better fitted to win. You then feel like you were filled with new strength. You give your best, and, against all expectations, you make it to the podium.

Thousands of eager mouths shout in unison, a piercing cry of joy. The crowd jubilates, chanting your name, hands outstretched to the sky. It is the homage and praise that your fans send you to salute your tremendous achievement and the joy you gave them. That is what Alleluia stands for. Wake up! It was just a dream, but now you understand what an Alleluia feels like, and you have experienced the adrenaline jolt this simple word can produce.

Alleluia is a cry, and it is also an exuberant expression of joy and happiness, a burst of joyfulness, a firework that illuminates the sky and puts exultation in all hearts.

Thank You O Lord My God

I remember a traditional Caribbean song that the great singer Harry Belafonte interpreted with talent. Powerful by its simplicity, it sounded like a cry to thank God for all his gifts and graces. The lyrics were filled with enthusiasm and devotion, humble abandonment, and gratitude for God's providence. This hymn of praise is probably inspired by the Book of Psalms, "The pasture is covered with sheep, and the valleys are clothed with wheat. The cries of joy and the songs resound." (Ps 65:9–13.) Here is the translation of this beautiful hymn:

> *Thank you, my Lord*
> *Look at all that nature has brought us.*
> *Thank you, my Lord,*
> *Look how misery has ended for us.*
> *The rain has fallen,*
> *The corn has grown,*

Ignore them and bear the consequences

All the children that were hungry will eat.
Let's chant,
Let's dance,
God in heaven,
That misery has ended for us.
Praise the Lord

You must praise the Lord to tell him how grateful you are for creating you and making you what you are, a wonderful person. The Scripture says, "I will praise thee; for I am fearfully and wonderfully made: marvelous are thy works; and that my soul knoweth right well." (Ps139:14) The Bible also says that we must praise the Lord because he is good and his mercy is eternal. God will always provide for the needs of his creatures. The Scripture says, "The Lord is my shepherd; I shall not want." (Ps 23:1). God is good, and his mercy is eternal. God will always provide for your needs; always provide your daily bread; always cause it to rain over the earth; always dress your wounds; always console your afflictions and your anguish, and he will always give you his blessing and protection.

God loves each one of his children as if they were his only child. The Scripture says "O give thanks unto the Lord; for he is good: because his mercy endureth for ever." (Ps 118:1.) The words inspired by this verse are found in 45 verses (1 Chr 16:34, 16:41, 2 Chr 5:13, 7: 3, 7: 6, 20:21, Ezr 3:11, Ps 106: 1; 107: 1, 118:1–4, 29, 136:1–16, Prv 22:18, 24:13–26, Jer 33:11). This is a good indication of the importance of these words, God is good, and his grace will never dry up! From God, your salvation will come. The Scripture says, "Salvation is of the Lord" (Jon 2:9).

Think about yourself; look at who you are and how you are. You are such a wonderful being. Do you realize how beautiful and intelligent you are? You are perfect to the point that you might be God's masterpiece. You have been chosen by the Lord, and he gave you birth. You will have his mercy forever. God is good, he is your shepherd, and you will never want. Your salvation will come from him, and he will be before you to transition you to your eternal life. Praise the Lord with your whole heart. Your supplication ought to be your personal masterpiece.

When Should You Praise the Lord?

You must praise the Lord before you begin a Supplication, but you must also do so during and after. A Supplication is not an ordinary prayer, learned in advance, or read from a prayer book, which you can say in a few minutes, between the moment you jump out of your bed and the moment you sit at the kitchen table to enjoy your breakfast. Supplications are acts of sincere devotion, which demand significant commitments.

The seven laws you will study in this essay must be understood, acknowledged, and carefully adhered to, should you want to elevate your soul towards God. For some believers, it will take little time, for they already have a healthy practice, but for others, it could take weeks or even months. If you have carefully followed, you understand that one of the crucial points implies that you must be led by faith, absolute faith, in God. You are also convinced that you have that faith if no doubt survives in your mind that God has given you what you need, even before making your request; Christ said, "For verily I say unto you, That whosoever shall say unto this mountain: be thou removed, and be thou cast into the sea; and shall not doubt in his heart, but shall believe that those things which he saith shall come to pass; he shall have whatsoever he saith." (Mk 11:23). And he said: "Therefore I say unto you, What things soever ye desire, when ye pray, believe that ye receive them, and ye shall have them."(Mk 11:24).

"And this is the confidence that we have in him, that, if we ask any thing according to his will, he heareth us: And if we know that he hear us, whatsoever we ask, we know that we have the petitions that we desired of him."(1 Jn 5:14–15). This is why it is necessary to address your praises of gratitude before you begin your supplication and before you are heard.

How can you expect to be heard if you are not convinced that God hears you? If your faith is not well established, do not ask; do not send him a supplication! God knows when you are not sincere, and when your confidence in him is faltering. You will not be heard by God simply because you ask for something. You will be heard when you demonstrate your trust in him, your firm commitment to accomplish His will, and the energy you devote to it. You must show that your whole being, your physical body, your ethereal body, your mind, and your soul altogether want to be heard by him.

If, when studying the seven biblical laws of supplication, you come across difficulties, your first reflex should be to seek guidance and confirmation from the Scriptures. In the book of psalms, for instance, you will find the divine inspiration and the help you are looking for. These precepts that inspired patriarchs and prophets will give you the same contentment, the same support. The Scriptures say: "Thy word is a lamp unto my feet, and a light unto my path." (Ps 119:105).

David had good reasons to be very worried about his life, for killers were on his heels. Rather than bemoan, he totally and assuredly put himself in the hands of God to seek his protection, and he calmly wrote this song, "I will sing of thy power; yea, I will sing aloud of thy mercy in the morning: for thou hast been my defense and refuge in the day of my trouble." (Ps 59:16).

David remained calm and praised the Lord, for he knew well that God listened to him and always responded to his supplications. David did not wait until after he had been heard to praise the Lord. He said, "I waited patiently for the Lord; and he inclined unto me, and heard my cry." (Ps 40:1).

Don't Go to God Empty-Handed

When you invoke God in Supplication, you are the petitioner! When invited by someone whom you value, or whom you would like to be close to, courtesy dictates you go with something in your hands, a little present you know will please them; Not necessarily an expensive one, but rather something you carefully chose for you knew it would be appreciated. This is called coming with your hands full. So, why do you think it is fine to go to God empty-handed? God, however, asks but little in comparison with what he has given you, and which he will continue to provide you with. The Scripture says, "Thus will I bless thee while I live: I will lift up my hands in thy name." (Ps 63:4).

When you go to God, hoping you will meet him and establish a lasting relationship with him, bring something! Offering him praises and thanksgiving before a Supplication is equivalent of going to him with a present in your hands.

If you believe without a shadow of a doubt that God will give you what you ask, you already have it. Whatever you ask in your supplications, be confident that you "have" received it, and you have it.

The Power of Chanting

When praising the Lord, there are two means of expression, uttering and chanting. Some prefer to use verbal expression, which

Ignore them and bear the consequences

is easier for them to understand. However, the words of human languages are limited in their ability to express all the nuances of feelings that must be conveyed while praising the Lord. Try to explain to someone the range of emotions you feel at some point. This is almost impossible, even using a rich and sophisticated vocabulary. The first difficulty is that you cannot identify all these feelings and define them precisely with words. Chanting brings to praising an extra semantic dimension particularly suited to express feelings. Therefore, if it is difficult to grasp the correct meaning of words, everything that is expressed through emotions instead of words is understood.

Chanting makes praises more devout and less talkative. Praises do not use words only. There are alternatives to words when you also want to convey to God your feelings and emotions. Words are for your exclusive use. They are like close captions that allow you to follow.

When your child is singing, while playing alone in his room, you realize that he is happy, content, and filled with joie de vivre. When, before falling asleep, he asks you to intone a lullaby, you understand that he wants to tell you how much your little one loves you. You comprehend that he wants to take your image in his dreams with him. However, if your child remains silent in his room, you worry, and you feel an urgent need to see if everything is going well. All this was accomplished without a word being exchanged; Without it being necessary to seek the right words. In this sense, chanting is a superior means of communication for expressing deep and varied feelings. A simple lullaby sung before he falls asleep has the power to calm a child who has trouble falling asleep and creates an unbreakable bond between him and you, the parent. Without using a single word, you have communicated a message to him, "you are for me, the being I love the most." And when he calms down and finally finds sleep, you know he understood your message. This is what you do when you praise the Lord. You say to him, "Lord, you are the most important being in my life, for you are my God."

You probably already noticed that when you sing with passion, you do not think of anything else. The worries, anxieties, and the never-ending questions which ordinarily burden your mind disappear as if by enchantment, to leave room for joy and exaltation. However, singing is not enough when praising the Lord. Songs take their source in your heart, while words come from your mind. This is why verbal expression and singing complement each other and must both be used to praise the Lord.

A third element is useful to exalt praise, music. In collective prayers, bands and choirs sometimes participate in the tribute of the faithful. While you praise God in the solitude of your supplication, why not creating a sound environment composed of your favorite music, classical music, sacred music, Beatles melodies, dance music such as salsa, which encourages the young and the elderly to improvise dance steps with no fear of ridicule. All types of music are suitable.

A few years ago, friends invited me to attend a service in New York City. When I saw the musicians and the vocalists settle on the small stage with their brass, percussions, and amplifiers, I wondered if I was at the right location. When the audience warmed up, singing the gospel to the sound of a blazing rhythm and blues, I sang with the audience, clapping my hands at the frantic pace of the music. The traditional "Praise the Lord!" appeared very pale and timid in comparison with those praises filled with emotions that I was witnessing. I felt such effervescence inside of me that I understood the profound meaning of the expression "Praise the Lord." I realized that when I praise the Lord with words, I speak to God; But when I add chanting while praising the Lord, using all the means of communication available, God talks back to me. He fills my heart with joy, happiness, and exaltation. What's essential at that moment is to belong totally to God, because no one can praise God if his heart is not wholly dedicated to him.

The psalmist sometimes addresses God to express his distress when facing certain afflictions, such as sickness, persecution, various calamities, or the feeling of having sinned, which can cause suffering. After expressing his distress, the psalmist begs God to help him, and his supplications are always accompanied with praise and thanksgiving, for he knows without a shadow of a doubt, that God has answered him. Unfailing faith is the very essence of Supplications; it is devotion in its purest form.

When you praise the Lord with words, you speak to Him; But when you sing your praises with all the means of expression at your disposal, God also speaks to you; He answers you and fills your heart with joy, happiness, and exaltation.

Praise and Thanksgiving

The Book of Psalms, which contains the God-inspired songs of praise to the Lord, occupies a central place in the Bible, and should always be at the forefront in the hearts of believers who praise the Lord. Like all Scriptures, the psalms are divinely inspired. Each psalm is written as a poem of great lyrical beauty. The psalms were sung to the sound of a harp or of a full orchestra. As the inspired word of God, the particular attributes of the psalms are also inspired by God, and therefore have the same importance as what composes them.

The psalms can be grouped into three groups: (1) the hymns of praise and thanksgiving that glorify the Lord for his goodness and mercy; (2) elegies, lyrical lamentations written simply, which cry out to God the distress and suffering of men, such as feelings of injustice, the guilt of sin, remorse, deep desire to confess sin, repentance, request for forgiveness, prayers of supplication; And (3) didactic psalms, imprecatory poems that give advice of justice and equity and stigmatize those who deviate from it.

In this essay on the Biblical laws of supplication, we will focus on the first group, and particularly on the hymns of praise and thanksgiving, for praise and thanksgiving are an integral part of the supplication. Their purpose is to glorify God for his goodness and for his mercy, which will never dry up. "I therefore exhort, above all things, to make prayers, supplications, petitions, and thanksgiving for all men. "(1 Tm 2: 1)

Everything has been given to you, and yet some look with disdain at all that God gave them as if the mere fact of having been born was enough reason to be given everything. Often, they feel they have not received enough or have received less than others, and they want more. Yet God owes you nothing, says the Bible "Who gave him first, so that he had to receive in return?" (Rom 11:35).

Offerings and Sacrifices

In antiquity, human sacrifice was the offering of choice among the neighboring nations of Israel. The firstborn was often destined to be sacrificed as an offering to their blood-greedy idols. The Bible testifies for such practices. Mesha, king of Moab, seeing he was undermined in a fight against Israel, sacrificed his own son to the gods of Moab. The Bible says, "Then he took his firstborn son, who was to reign in his stead, and offered him as a burnt offering on the wall." (2 Kgs 3:27). So, did Ahaz the son of Jotham, of whom the Bible says, "He caused his son to pass by fire" (2 Kgs 16: 3, 2 Chr 28: 3) Manasseh succeeded his father, Hezekiah, when he was only 12 years old. During his reign, he departed from God and renewed himself with the worship of idols. He rebuilt all

Ignore them and bear the consequences

the altars which his father had destroyed and re-established the forbidden occult practices. The Scripture says, "He [Manasseh] caused his son to pass by fire; He observed the clouds and the serpents to draw prognosis, and he set up people who called on spirits and predicted the future" (2 Kgs 21: 6). Ezekiel denounced these practices. The Bible says, "By presenting your offerings, by passing your children through the fire, you still defile yourself today with all your idols." (Ez 20:31). Jeremiah also rebelled. The Scripture says, "The idols have devoured the produce of the work of our fathers, from our youth, their sheep and their oxen, their sons and their daughters" (Jer 3:24–25).

The psalter reveals the extent of the practices of the immolation of children on the altar of idols and false gods. The Scripture says: "They sacrificed their sons and daughters to idols" (Ps 106: 37), "They shed innocent blood, the blood of their sons and daughters, whom they sacrificed to the idols of Canaan" (Ps 106: 38). These horrible murders took place everywhere. The Scripture also says: "Warming up near the terebinths, under every green tree, slaughtering the children in the valleys, under cracks of rocks" (Is 57: 5).

For the perpetrator of such acts, the consequences were often immediate and painful. When the Israelites were attacked by the Ammonites, Jephthah, who had been appointed to lead the battle against the Ammonites, invoked the Lord and vowed that if he came out victorious in this battle he would offer as a holocaust the first person who would cross the threshold of his home to welcome him upon his return home. When he returned a victor, he was greeted by his daughter, his only daughter, whom he cherished more than anyone else. She crossed the threshold of his home, accompanied by music and dances. Then, the Scripture says, "He [Jephthah] fulfilled upon her the vow which he had made." (Jgs 11:39).

God put Abraham to the test by giving him an order. "Take your son, your only one, the one you love, Isaac; [...] and offer him for a holocaust" (Gn 22: 2). Abraham did not revolt. He did not even question the divine order. He prepared without delay to carry out God's commandment. Abraham, who had renounced idolatrous cults by his own volition, was no stranger to their practices, which his people found hard to abandon.

Among neighboring peoples, the immolation of the firstborn was a common practice for those who wished to obtain the graces of their gods. Why then did God ask Abraham to submit to a tradition derived from idolatrous cults? Was it merely to put his faith to the test? Certainly not! God subjected his most faithful servant to this terrible ordeal, to serve as an example to the people of Israel and to all their descendants. But God stopped Abraham's arm before it hit his son Isaac. The divine message was clear; human sacrifices must stop! Stop immolating your sons and daughters! The offering of a ram or other animal is sufficient. I accepted that Abraham would substitute the immolation of an animal for that of his eldest son, and I will also allow it to you. This divine intervention resulted in the gradual abandonment of human sacrifices, which God did not love. The Bible says, "Thou shalt not do so with the LORD thy God; For they served their gods by doing all the abominations that are odious to the LORD, and they burned their sons and their daughters with fire in honor of their gods in the fire" (Dt 12:31).

This alternative was gradually accepted by the people of Abraham, but the practice of blood sacrifices judged superior to the vegetable offerings, spread to excess. Through the prophets, God imposed severe constraints on the rules of the ritual immolation of animals. He decreed that the sacrifices, which took place everywhere and, in all circumstances, could only be done at the tabernacle, and later at the temple. He then decreed that only priests could immolate sacrificial animals. Then God set the tone, and said, "I will strike them by the prophets" (Hos 6: 5).

Through the mouth of the prophets, God made known how much he disliked this useless bloodshed. The Lord never tarried at these giant barbecues, not that he was choosy, but because God does not feed on earthly foods. God said, "I love piety and not sacrifices, and knowledge of God more than holocausts." (Hos 6:6.) "Though ye offer me burnt offerings and your meat offerings, I will not accept them" (Am 5:22). Through Isaiah, God said, "What have I to do with the multitude of your sacrifices?" (Is 1:11.) By the mouth of Jeremiah, God spoke thus: "Your burnt offerings do not please me, and your sacrifices are not agreeable to me" (Jer 6:20), and by the voice of Malachi, He insisted, "I have no pleasure in you, saith the Lord of hosts, neither will I accept an offering at your hand." (Mal 1:10). David said, "If you had wanted sacrifices, I would have offered you; But you do not take pleasure in holocausts" (Ps 51:16). Isaiah endeavored to explain these useless massacres of animals did not please God, and that they were not sufficient. The Scripture says, "Lebanon is not enough for fire, and its animals are not enough for the burnt offering" (Is 40:16). The people of God understood through the action of the prophets what was pleasing to God, observing his laws, the study of the Scriptures, prayer, the practice of justice, equity, and mercy. The Scripture says: "Obedience is better than sacrifices, and the observation of his word is better than the fat of rams" (1 Sm 15:22) The Bible reveals what God inspired to Solomon: "The sacrifice of the wicked is abhorrent to the Lord, but the prayer of the upright is agreeable to him" (Prv 15: 8). "To do justice and judgment is more acceptable to the Lord than sacrifice." (Prv 21: 3). The psalmist explains what is pleasing to the Lord; God prefers the attitude of the repentant sinner who comes to him with a broken spirit and a broken heart. The Scripture says,

"The sacrifices of God are a broken spirit: a broken and a contrite heart, O God, thou wilt not despise." (Ps 51:17). And "Offer unto God thanksgiving" (Ps 50:14). And Prophet Micah reveals that neither money nor material goods are of a nature to please God, for God possesses everything; He has no material need. If this were the case, the rich could redeem their sins more effortlessly than the humble. Moreover, an offering destined to God must necessarily be commensurable with His Majesty. Should the life of his own son be offered to please God? Error! For it would be to redeem his sins by committing an even greater one. The Scripture says, "With what shall I present myself before God, to humble myself before the Most High God? Shall I present myself with burnt offerings, with calves a year old? Will the Lord accept thousands of rams, myriads of torrents of oil? Shall I give for my transgressions my firstborn, for the sin of my soul the fruit of my womb? You have been made known, O man, what is good; And what the Lord requires of you is that you practice righteousness, love mercy, and walk humbly with your God" (Mi 6:6–8). The prophets perceived the necessity of a superior offering, which would be composed neither of material goods nor of human or animal flesh. By their mouth, God had clearly spoken against this offering. Even the offering of a firstborn, the dearest being in the heart of every man, was considered by God as an offense. How, under these conditions, offer God a commensurable sacrifice with His Majesty, and with our immense need to show him our fidelity? The dilemma lasted a long time until a man endowed with a tremendous love for his fellow men accomplished what no one before him had done. He offered himself as an offering to God, not to obtain any personal benefit, but to redeem the sins of his fellow men.

The Bible says, "Walk in charity, following the example of Christ, who loved us, and gave himself up to God for us as an offering and sacrifice of good odor" (Eph 5:2).

Christ, through his ultimate sacrifice, made to God the offering of his own person for the good of others. "He [Christ] entered once and for all into the most holy place, not with the blood of goats and calves, but with his own blood, having obtained eternal redemption." (Heb 9:12).

A Gift from God

The Bible presents salvation as a gift from God to those with faith in him and who obey his laws and commandments. "The salvation of the righteous comes from the Lord" (Ps 37:39) "By grace you are saved by means of faith. And this does not come from you, it is the gift of God." (Eph 2:8–9).

The Bible says: Entrust your soul to God as an offering. He will fill it with his blessing, and you will gain in reward salvation and eternal life, in sanctification. "It is in God that my soul confides; From him comes my salvation." (Ps 62: 2.)

Joy and Happiness

Joy and happiness express absolute faith in God. This faith results from the acceptance of the state of utter dependence of humans towards their creator. Contentment and cheerfulness cannot, however, be expressed absent happiness. Happiness precedes pleasure and joyfulness. But where does happiness come from? The Bible says: "He who trusts in the Lord is happy" (Prv 16:20). Happiness is, therefore, the result of a successful relationship with God. A couple is happy when their union is cloudless. A teacher is glad when he has conquered the confidence of his students, who absorb his teachings without doubting his credibility. A child is happy when he knows he is loved. A dog is happy when he does not feel the anxiety of being abandoned by those he loves. A believer is thrilled when he has fulfilled his quest for God and has established a strong and unfailing personal relationship with him. The Bible says, "There are abundant joys before your face" (Ps 16:11).

The psalmist asks, "Who will show us happiness?" (Ps 4: 6.) But in the following verse, he reveals that he knows well the answer to his questions: "You put more joy in my heart than they have when their wheat and their moth abound" (Ps 4: 7).

Happiness is the essence of life. God sends his gifts and blessings to his creatures, and they respond by manifesting to the Creator their joy to be so much loved. Through their demonstrations of joy and happiness, they bear witness to the existence and strength of their sacred relationship with their Creator.

But beware! Happiness is not selfish; It is a gift of God supposed to be shared, like all other divine gifts. Happiness is only consecrated if it is shared with the highest number of others. The Bible says, "Thou shalt rejoice thy son, and thy daughter, and thy servant, and thy handmaid, the Levite that shall be in thy gates, and the stranger, the orphan, and the widow that are in the midst of thee." (Dt 16:11).

Affliction, sadness, suffering, anxiety, is not conducive to supplication. Those who suffer from disorders will struggle in their quest of God, for ailment indicates the absence of faith. The Scripture says: "I trust in thy loving kindness, I have joy in the heart, because of thy salvation" (Ps 13: 5).

Anxiety, fear of the morrow, is the source of all afflictions. But placing your trust in God and being guided in your choices only by the intense desire to fulfill His Will, are the two behaviors that generate happiness. The Bible says: "Young man, rejoice in your youth, deliver your heart to joy during the days of your youth" (Eccl 11: 9) God hears the one who comes to him with his heart filled with joy and happiness, for happiness is the design of man, as God willed it.

The Bible says, "Be glad and rejoice in the LORD your God." (Jl 2:23.) "Serve the LORD with gladness: come before his presence with singing." (Ps 100:2)

Happiness is the fruit of behaviors that contributes to fulfilling the Divine Will. When your practice pleases God, God anoints you with his blessing and fills your heart with happiness. "God takes pleasure in what you do." (Eccl 9:7.) These moments of intense joy are propitious to Supplication. They are like windows that open to the Divine Light. In these blessed moments, you will feel how close God is to you.

Wake up! Refuse to be one of those who have no faith, "I know thy works, that thou hast a name that thou livest, and art dead." (Rv 3:1) Follow David's example, instead. The Scripture says, "Awake up, my glory; awake, psaltery and harp: I myself will awake early. I will praise thee, O Lord, among the people: I will sing unto thee among the nations." (Ps 57:8–9).

Salvation as a gift from God to those with faith in him and who obey his laws and commandments. The salvation of the righteous comes from the Lord. Entrust your soul to God as an offering. He will fill it with his blessing, and you will gain in reward salvation and eternal life, in sanctification.

The Bible says, "It is in God that my soul confides; From him comes my salvation." (Ps 62:2.)

Law #6
The Law of Elevation

"The glory of the Lord shall be thy reward." (Is 58: 8)

What Does Elevation Mean?

How can one explain what an elevation is to someone who has never experienced it? It is easier to say everything that Elevation is not than what it is. It is not a self-improvement method to enhance your self-confidence. It is not a psychological technique to increase your powers of concentration. It is not a new age method of introspection or meditation, and much less a mind control or thought reforming technique. An Elevation is neither a method nor an operating procedure. It is the opposite of all that. An Elevation is the ascent of a soul attempting to draw near to God, an essential phase in a Supplication. Elevation cannot be practiced independently of the Supplication.

The Bible says, "Draw nigh to God, and he will draw nigh to you." (Jas 4:8a).

Before you study this biblical law, make sure that you understand the other precepts developed in the previous chapters of this book, and that you are exclusively driven by faith. Also, make sure that you have attempted an earnest and sufficient effort at sanctification. Trying to raise your soul to the Lord without having fulfilled the requirement of sanctification could be an offense to the Lord.

The Bible says, "Cleanse your hands, ye sinners; and purify your hearts, ye double minded." (Jas 4:8b)

The Elevation is the ascent of the soul of someone who seeks the Lord and tries to draw near to him. It is a significant phase of a Supplication. You elevate yourself when you raise your soul to God to meet him, to know him, and to establish a personal and lasting relationship with him. The Scripture says, "Whilst we are at home in the body, we are absent from the Lord" (2 Cor 5:6b).

Job's Trying Ordeal

God had given everything to Job, for he regarded him as the most perfect of his servants. But God took back everything he had given him. After having reclaimed all properties and chattels, God removed his children away from him; And God took away from him the love and trust of his wife and that of his servants. Finally, God reclaimed the last thing Job still possessed, his good health. "Naked came I out of my mother's womb, and naked shall I return thither: The Lord gave, and the Lord hath taken away; blessed be the name of the Lord." (Jb 1:21).

Could it be conceivable that God had been unfair toward His most perfect servant? No! God can't be unjust! Despite his notable perfection, Job had committed two faults, which he had never tried to correct. He believed he was perfect since he had been so exceptionally blessed by the Lord; that was his first mistake. Only the Lord can decide if someone is perfect. That, Job would learn it later, helped by the brilliant mind of the young Elihu.

However, Job's greatest mistake was that he had never attempted to raise his soul to God and establish a personal relationship with him. Job had never felt the need for it, for he had always received everything from the Lord without ever having to ask. Throughout his life, Job had always scrupulously observed all laws, decrees, and divine commandments to the letter. He was charitable and generous, honest, and respectful, he loved God and feared him, but something was missing for his faith to be perfect. He had never felt the need to know God better. He never supplicated to the Lord, and he never endeavored to ascend and go to him. After he lost everything; After the death of his children; After having several times thought of committing suicide; After having been humiliated by his so-called "friends"; After having lost the esteem of his wife and of his faithful servants; And after having, at the instigation of his "friends" and accusers, examined one by one all the sins he could have committed, but which he was sure he never committed; Then, at last, he understood, and, turning to the Lord, he pronounced what would secure his redemption: "I have heard of thee by the hearing of the ear: but now mine eye seeth thee." (Jb 42:5).

Job could have started earlier in his life his quest for God and the Elevation of his soul to get closer to the Lord and to forge with him a lasting personal relationship, by elevating himself through a Supplication. He would not have suffered so much. His quest for God and his desire to ascend to him, to raise his soul to the Lord and come near to Him, Job accomplished it belatedly through pain and suffering, for Job had always believed that he was perfect. Had he been faultless, he was not dispensed from asserting his trust in God by going to him through the Elevation of his soul through Supplication. All his life, Job had demonstrated how much he feared God and how much he loved him, but he had never shown how absolute his faith was. Supplications are essential acts of devotion that the Lord wants to hear.

However, God allowed Job to repair his blunder, but then,

at the cost of unimaginable suffering. These sufferings were not meant to punish Job for sins he had committed, but because God loved the most perfect of all his servants, he wanted to give him a second chance he deserved and open his eyes.

When you have successfully accomplished your own elevation, like Job, you'll say, I had heard of you by word of mouth, my Lord, but now I see you with my own eyes.

Your Jacob's Ladder

Jacob had a dream in which a ladder appeared to him. The Bible says: "He dreamed, and behold a ladder set up on the earth, and the top of it reached to heaven: and behold the angels of God ascending and descending on it" (Gn 28:12). He saw the image of God standing above the ladder. The Bible says: "The Lord stood above it, and said, I am the Lord God of Abraham thy father, and the God of Isaac: the land whereon thou liest, to thee will I give it, and to thy seed" (Gn 28:13). Jacob had the intuition that God wanted him to understand that the allegory of the ladder meant there existed a means that Jacob could use to communicate with him.

You have set your foot on the first step of your ladder when you read this essay. You even climbed several more steps when you studied the first biblical laws of Supplication. Your efforts towards sanctification have led you even much higher on your ladder. You successfully fought against the gravitational forces that pushed you down to earth. However, you are not ready yet for the last leg of your journey, at the conclusion of which you will find yourself in the presence of God, says the Bible. "Ye shall seek me, and find me, when ye shall search for me with all your heart. And I will be found of [by] you, saith the Lord." (Jer 29:13–14).

At this point in your quest, God has noticed your commendable efforts, and even if you go no further, rest assured that you are no longer, in his eyes, a number in a crowd. You are already part of a small elite of chosen ones that God wants to have near to him, that he will not forsake.

The Bible says: "Thou, Lord, hast not forsaken them that seek thee." (Ps 9:10). And the Lord said, "I love them that love me; and those that seek me early shall find me." (Prv 8:17). If you continue your journey to your destination, God will stand by you. He will help you by making himself easily discoverable by you when the time comes. The Bible says: "The Lord shall guide thee continually" (Is 58:11a). If all this seems hard to comprehend, don't be uneasy because by seeking God, you will understand everything. "They that seek the Lord understand all things" (Prv 28: 5).

Remember, above all, that once you have vowed to commit yourself to the Lord, you cannot go back without offending him, and those who offend God will face the consequences, according to the Bible. "Better is it that thou shouldest not vow, than that thou shouldest vow and not pay" (Eccl 5: 5).

Knowing Good and Evil

You may still wonder why you need to elevate yourself to God, when you just wanted to supplicate to the Lord, hoping that he would hear your requests. The answer to your questions is in the first pages of the Bible.

When God created man, they did not differ from other animal species. Like them, man lived naked and was not ashamed of his nakedness, for he was not conscious of it. Like all animals, man relied on the divine providence for all his needs. He lived in an environment where food was plentiful and readily available. A

Ignore them and bear the consequences

paradisiacal situation, if so. It is not unreasonable to think that during the early ages of creation, men did not differ from animals. Horses never felt the need to learn a trade, to plow fields, or to sow and harvest. Horses feed on grass, which covers the whole earth. The Bible says: "Behold the fowls of the air: for they sow not, neither do they reap, nor gather into barns; yet your heavenly Father feedeth them. Are ye not much better than they?" (Mt 6:26). .

Birds are not even concerned about stocking food for later, so much do they trust the Divine Providence. Men only had to stretch out his arm to pick a fruit from a tree or a plant on the side of the way. Absent conscience, the divine providence provided them with everything they needed. But God had a higher design for man, and for it to be accomplished, men had to learn of the exceptional abilities which the Lord had endowed him with, and he had to accept in all awareness the purpose that God had assigned to him.

The biblical author used a very poetic metaphor to describe this critical moment when men ceased to be nothing other than biological animals to become superior creatures, not only capable of understanding God's Will but of fulfilling it willfully. Although this metaphor is beautiful, it is also enigmatic. It has intrigued many generations of believers, and to this day, no unanimous consensus satisfies modern men's need for rationality.

In Genesis, the serpent had with Eve a short and apparently innocent conversation, which had a significant impact on the future of the human species. This conversation is responsible for the most significant paradigm shift that men have ever experienced. "The serpent was more subtle than any beast of the field which the Lord God had made. And he said unto the woman, Yea, hath God said, Ye shall not eat of every tree of the garden? And the woman said unto the serpent, we may eat of the fruit of the trees of the garden: But of the fruit of the tree which is in the midst of the garden, God hath said, Ye shall not eat of it, neither shall ye touch it, lest ye die. And the serpent said unto the woman, Ye shall not surely die: For God doth know that in the day ye eat thereof, then your eyes shall be opened, and ye shall be as gods, knowing good and evil." (Gn 3:1–5).

I will not dwell on the serpent's role narrated in Genesis. Who was this serpent? Was his species subtler than the human species at creation? Was he the symbolic representation of a heavenly entity, an angel, for instance? Was he, on the contrary, the incarnation of Satan, who, perfidiously, took advantage of the woman's innocence to incite her to yield to temptation and commit the irreparable? God had forbidden humans to consume the fruit of the tree of knowledge, but by evoking a false reason: "lest you die" (Gn 3: 3). As for the serpent, acknowledge that he revealed only the truth: "And the serpent said unto the woman, Ye shall not surely die: For God doth know that in the day ye eat thereof, then your eyes shall be opened, and ye shall be as gods, knowing good and evil." (Gn 3:4–5). Does this mean that God wanted men to be ignorant? Hard to believe, I will leave it to exegetes and theologians to discuss this critical but perplexing subject. I am inclined to think that the role of the serpent was of capital importance for the future of man, and what matters here are the consequences of these acts.

After God found that the first human couple had transgressed His instructions and eaten the forbidden fruit, He was disappointed, but He accepted it, like a father who hears for the first time that his child did something wrong. However, God did not accuse the serpent of having lied. He simply reprimanded him for not keeping his mouth shut, and for revealing a truth that He had no intent to disclose to men yet. It reminds me of a situation that many parents have had to face. They want to protect their teenage daughter from temptations, and unwanted influences, for she is too young and too innocent to know how to defend herself. Their insistence is often experienced as tyranny by their child if she doesn't understand this has nothing to do with oppression or abuse of power. Is it not all parents' desire to become, one day, grandparents?

The Bible says: "Be fruitful and multiply" (Gn 1:28b; 9:7a). "Bring forth abundantly in the earth, and multiply therein." (Gn 9:7b).

Like any good father, God was waiting for the moment he thought fit to reveal to Adam and Eve the plan he had for them and the exceptional powers he had endowed upon them so they could fulfill their mission. He would have lifted the veil gradually, but the impudent serpent hastened things. From now on, men must face a new reality; they discover that they are far more than animals. They realize that by creating them in his image, God had also placed his Spirit in them, a particle of divinity which makes them like God, mindful beings with heavenly talents, who can discern good from evil. "The Lord God said, Behold, the man is become as one of us, to know good and evil" (Gn 3:22a). After this statement, the Lord's reaction was to show his anger and to punish his disobedient children, but like any good father, the punishments were mitigated. To the woman, "In sorrow thou shalt bring forth children." (Gn 3:16); And to the man, "In the sweat of thy face shalt thou eat bread" (Gn 3:19a). Then our first ancestors were driven out of the garden of Eden, says the Scripture. "Therefore the Lord God sent him forth from the garden of Eden, to till the ground from whence he was taken." (Gn 3:23).

But was it really a punishment? We have seen earlier that God's will means working with Him as partners, so his creation will continue and thrive forever. God wants men and all creatures to work in harmony to ensure the sustainability of his beautiful work. Didn't God promise to send rain, which is essential to sustain life, on the condition that men and all other creatures also contribute to their work, so the creation may thrive forever? "Who giveth rain upon the earth, and sendeth waters upon the fields" (Jb 5:10).

God said to Adam, "Cursed is the ground for thy sake" (Gn 3:17); but did he curse the ground? No, for he later said, "I will give you rain in due season, and the land shall yield her increase, and the trees of the field shall yield their fruit." (Lv 26: 4)..

Like a good father, God saw his children leave the Garden of Eden, where they had lived happily. Men were now faced with their responsibilities. Now on their own and autonomous, they had to make sure they would not stray from the path of God, and that they would always seek him, like a child who visits his parents after becoming an adult. You, the man the Lord made in his image, the godlike man who knows good and evil, God wants you to go closer to him, again and again, and to drink at his source. God made you in his image; he wants you to care for His image and to remain like Him.

The Sprinter

In my college years, I had a good Canadian friend, a college athlete extremely gifted in his specialty, the 100 meters. He sometimes invited me to attend his practices and training. I asked him how he prepared for competing. His answer stood in three words: Practice! Practice! Practice! He explained that drill consumed most of the time he devoted to the sport, and he added that there was something more to win a race. Before the race, said he, I listen to the advice of my teammates. My coach knows my strengths and weaknesses. He gives me last-minute instructions. My teammates tell me about the athletes I will face, their strong points, and their techniques.

The desire to withdraw from the competition briefly comes

to my mind, did he say. But when I get farther away from the locker room and closer to the track, my team and their advice are no longer in my mind. I am alone. I muster my strength, and I think about what I have to accomplish in ten seconds. I don't even think about my opponents.

When I am on the starting line, I no longer think of anything else. My goal is the only thing I can think of. Reaching the finish line in 10 seconds, running as fast as I can. Even if I am ahead of the group, it's not enough; I must surpass myself, I must go over and above my own limits. I don't care about beating the others yet; I only care about doing better than I have ever done before.

During the first half of the race, I think of the technique, and I focus on breathing. I try to maintain a regular pace, without giving my best effort yet, because the moment has not come to make the last effort. I must keep enough energy for the end. But, when I see the finish line, it's not my legs nor my muscles that count to lead me to win, it's my head. I feel like my body is too heavy, and this weight will prevent me from winning. I must take an extra step. Thus, my head takes over the commands and erases my body. I no longer feel my muscles, my legs, or my feet. I feel like I'm flying. In my head, all ideas converge towards one sole goal: to win! Any thought not meant to lead me to victory is a parasitic idea, and I expel it from my brain in a flash. I no longer feel the slightest pain or stiffness because my physical body no longer exists. I am the best sprinter in the world and nothing can stop me from winning. If the sequence of mental events happens appropriately, I know whether I'll be on the podium. As soon as my body has been erased, I feel the finish line is running like a rocket towards me. My legs have nothing more to do to win the race; I'm no longer aware of their existence. It's my head that causes me to succeed.

Years later, I can't help but think that the practice of an extreme sport like competition level racing has something in common with an Elevation during a Supplication. To win a race, you don't start when you are setting foot on the starting line. To win a race, you begin a few years earlier, when you learn to run, gain muscle and velocity, and compete against other budding athletes. You reach another level when you realize that persistence and willpower are two essential assets if you want to reach a finish line one day. To achieve this, you set to yourself modest goals you can make in the short term. Then you set goals that are higher and more difficult to reach, with patience and stubbornness.

The Bible says, "Know ye not that they which run in a race run all, but one receiveth the prize? So run, that ye may obtain." (1 Cor 9:24). Every tenth of a second of improvement over his last performance was a great victory for my friend, and repeating such a performance was an even higher achievement. It's important to remember that all the other competitors prepare themselves in the same way, but only one will cross the finish line a winner.

As a believer, you ought to climb one by one the steps of your own Jacob's ladder, with patience and perseverance. You were not meant to stay put on the ground. God assigned a specific purpose to your life. Start moving up when you understand the Will of God, and why you must elevate yourself and get nearer to God.

The Noises

The repetitive prayers and the strict adherence to beliefs and practices that some churches impose on their faithful are prone to generating degrees of anxiety and guilt, leading to behaviors that rather belong to superstition than to authentic faith. The believer feels guilty of not having performed a ritual correctly, of having modified a rite that he was supposed to observe carefully, of having violated a rule imposed upon him by his church, although his own rationale is reluctant to agree with it. The believer may think that his behavior might bring him misfortune or that something unpleasant might happen to him.

Too strict rules and stringent creed may turn honest beliefs into obsessions. Obsessions are parasitic thoughts that invade and perturb people's mind, preventing them from thinking correctly and focusing effectively. These parasitic thoughts sometimes drive you to submit yourself to an oppressive ritual. You can check if it ever happened to you. When, for instance, you walk on a sidewalk or tiled floor, have you ever felt a conscious or unconscious impulse to land your feet always in the exact same place, either at the center of the tiles, on their edge, or on one corner?

These persistent, intrusive, and dominating thoughts appear, sometimes, in images that impose themselves onto your mind. These parasitic images are hard to dismiss. When you think that you got rid of them, they come back again and again. People affected by this syndrome can't reason and focus regularly. Physicians call that affliction "obsessive-compulsive disorder."

Many people have been affected by this syndrome, and a few can get rid of these mental nuisances by themselves. Those who are more affected by this problem should seek the help of a therapist. But, unfortunately, many prefer to keep it to themselves. They try to accommodate it to the best of their ability, fearing to expose it to others, for they might see it as a weakness, at least, or a mental disorder, at worst.

Thus, some give in to the irrepressible urges to wash their hands more frequently than necessary; Others give in to a need to check all the time if the windows are closed before going to bed; Still, others believe they can live a healthy life, although they are affected by a compulsion to repeat certain words, like, for instance, the last words of the sentence which they have just pronounced; How many struggle with offensive images, blasphemous or obscene thoughts, that continuously appear in their mind? All these noises that disturb the mind and hinder the establishment of a good relationship with God must be eliminated or at least kept in check and mastered during elevation.

Fearing God

Obsolete religious education methods of yesteryear based on the irrational fear of God and the prospect of severe punishment for those who don't carefully abide by the mandatory rites imposed onto the believer by some denominations affected many generations of believers. They lost their ability to think by themselves willfully, and on their own free will. This is not what the Bible teaches. The Bible does not teach to fear God. The Bible teaches to love God like a child loves his father. "Thou shalt love the Lord thy God with all thine heart, and with all thy soul, and with all thy might." (Dt 6:5, 4:29, 10:12, 26:16, 30: 2, 30: 6, 30:10, Mt 22:37, Mk 12:30, Lk 10:27). "There is no fear in love; but perfect love casteth out fear: because fear hath torment. He that feareth is not made perfect in love." (1 Jn 4:18). The Bible does not say that God wants to subdue us by fear; On the contrary, it teaches that God loves us as we love our children. "Behold, what manner of love the Father hath bestowed upon us, that we should be called the sons of God." (1 Jn 3:1).

The Bible says that when Abraham moved to sacrifice his son Isaac, the angel of God stopped his gesture. "Now I know that thou fearest God" (Gn 22:12). The "fear of God" is an expression frequently found in the Bible. However, the Hebrew verb "Yare," used in the original texts, has several meanings. It may mean "fearing," but it also expresses moral fear, respect for authority, and a sense of honor, such as, for instance, how one feels towards one's parents or a highly respected moral authority. In the Scripture, "Now I know that thou fearest God" suggests that Abraham had not been influenced by the fear of God, but rather by his deep love and respect for the Lord.

Being Heard by God

Nowadays, some churches still advocate the use of formulas based on acronyms, or words formed from the initial letters of a series of words that compose a phrase. The advantage of using such abbreviations lies in the fact that they are an excellent mnemonic means for remembering a short text or a series of words. However, acronyms, if they favor the memorization of short concepts, focus attention on a minimal number of words, to the detriment of much broader ideas, that are more important than the simple memorization of a few words in the right order. People subjected to these methods in their teens, confess their confusion when, in adulthood, they remember the acronym but forgot what it meant. Spirituality thus limited to the few keywords that make up the abbreviation can be summed up as hollow and meaningless rituals that avoid appealing to the mind and spirit of the believer, and that forbid, to whom seeks God, using the means of intelligent search, which the Bible teaches to foster.

The Bible says, "Be ye not as the horse, or as the mule, which have no understanding." (Ps 32:9)

Renounce using hollow magic formulas, so-called proven methods, and magic recipes. Leave magic formulas to magicians and secret recipes to sorcerers' apprentices. Supplications are long and hard journeys that can have no shortcuts, like conquest expeditions. They are more like struggles of which you hope you'll be victorious. You will only succeed if you take an active and positive role in your mission.

Supplications are mostly silent except when praising God and expressing joy and happiness. The words of human languages are not useful to those who want to be heard by God, for God probes the hearts and minds of everyone. The Bible says, "There is not a word in my tongue, but, lo, O Lord, thou knowest it altogether." (Ps 139:4). God hears the supplications of the righteous, even when they are silent. The virtuous man is assured to be heeded by God, and his Supplications are satisfied.

The Bible speaks of Anne, Elkana's wife, who was barren and so wished to have a child. She went to the Temple, where she addressed a supplication to the Lord, speaking in her heart said, "Now Hannah, she spake in her heart; only her lips moved, but her voice was not heard: therefore, Eli thought she had been drunken." (1 Sm 1:13). Eli saw her do it, but he did not understand what she was doing. She remained prostrate for a long time. He found it very strange that her lips moved, but that no sound came out of it. He even thought that Anne was sick or she had lost her head. He approached her to look closely at her behavior, and when she got up he asked her what she was doing. And she said to him, "I have poured out my soul before the Lord." (1 Sm 1:15). God, however, heard Anne's fervent and silent supplication, for she bore a son; "Wherefore it came to pass, when the time was come about after Hannah had conceived, that she bare a son" (1 Sm 1:20).

Ignore them and bear the consequences

Spiritual Convergence

During the Elevation phase of a Supplication, you'll put your thoughts in good order as you want them to converge like a laser beam towards a single subject. Spiritual convergence is the act of focusing dynamically on a single thought while praying, ignoring all parasitic feelings that could interfere with your attempt to create a stable personal relationship with God. Hence, few words are necessary, for your prayer no longer needs to cover ambient noises. "A fool's voice is known by multitude of words." (Eccl 5:3)

When you are awake, your mind is continuously busy with conscious activities like thinking, understanding, learning, and memorizing. Your intellect receives a continuous flow of thousands of data it processes at high speed, sorting and classifying, analyzing, matching with data already stored in your memory, and the result is immediately provided to you. The brain, an indefatigable computer, is always active and can even handle several simultaneous chains of events. That's an excellent thing because this overflowing activity allows you to lead a healthy life. On any day of your life, you learn things; You remember things you learned long ago; You enrich your experience; You solve multiple problems that pop-up in your mind with no warning, small household problems, and complex existential problems; Your brain analyzes the data it receives, and you understand what happens to you; You decide; You solve problems; You think about what you should do to help your children make progress in mathematics; You have an emotional thought for a deceased loved one; You make your prayers and praise the Lord; etc. All this being done simultaneously and with no efforts, because your brain knows how to take things in hand in an autonomous way. However, that's where the problem lies.

You probably know this true story, the story of an entrepreneur who hired a highly qualified employee, perhaps a little bit overqualified though. The new recruit was so professional and so competent that he was promoted to the position of Chief Executive Officer, so he had become the right-hand man of the boss. This employee was hardworking, experienced, and very active. He did not need to be told what to do because he knew it already, and he could make the right decisions quicker than his boss.

The entrepreneur entrusted him with more responsibilities. Hence, the entrepreneur could spend more and more time on vacation or away from his desk while making more money. He was so pleased that he hired this employee he praised him all around. He thought, once, of offering him a higher salary, but, after thinking twice about it, he postponed the decision because he had not asked for it. One day, the model employee received a hiring proposal from a competitor. That offer was of the kind he could not refuse. Our greedy entrepreneur felt disoriented. He now had to relearn his trade, his market, how to operate his own company, and even the names of his employees. He had forsaken the control of his business for so long that he was now overwhelmed by the simple task of managing his small business and unable to decide. He filed for bankruptcy. Now, you understand why you must always keep control of your thoughts and let no one take control of your mind and tell you how you should think and what you should do.

These activities that keep your mind active on a full-time basis are beneficial, even essential for you, but when they occupy your entire wake time, how much time remains for your relationship with God? This is the question. When you are well engaged in an elevation, and you are about to know the unique experience of an encounter with God, and you are disturbed by a phone ringing, the children fighting and the deadline for filing your taxes, can you rely on the model employee who resides in your head to solve all these problems? You are not in the ideal conditions to reconnect with God. What could you do to escape this spiral of mental turbulence that prevents you from devoting yourself entirely to God, even if only for a moment?

The sequels of the past, on the one hand, and the uncertainties of the future are the two most severe causes of stress and anxiety, and they are responsible for all your miseries. From your past come these predicaments: the feeling of failure; The lack of self-confidence; Guilt; Grudge; Bereavement; Childhood diseases and their possible sequels; Relational snags; etc. These various disorders weaken your immune, physiological, and mental systems, leaving you defenseless when facing all kinds of physical or psychosomatic attacks.

But anxiety, fear, depression, sadness, dread, insecurity, etc., come from the anguish of the future. Somatization is a psychological process that transforms emotional difficulties into functional disorders: headaches, migraines, rheumatism, digestive disorders, skin disorders, panic attacks, depression, etc.

Anxiety does not provide you with solutions for the future; however, it deprives you today of the strength and energy you need to overcome your afflictions effectively. To keep these problems from the past and the future far away, reply to the present moment and see how you will feel relaxed and more serene.

According to the Bible, this particle of divinity, which God has placed in you "The spirit that dwelleth in us" (Jas 4:5). gives you the power to achieve sanctification all by yourself, to raise your soul toward God and to achieve the purpose God assigned to your life, that is fulfilling God's will. God possesses, in your heart, a permanent residence.

The Bible says: "What? know ye not that your body is the temple of the Holy Ghost which is in you,

**which ye have of God, and ye are not your own?"
(1 Cor 6:19).**

God is present in the heart of all his children. If only you knew how to be received in this temple in you, deep within your inner being, to meet him, talk to him, ask him for help to relieve your suffering, and calm your anxieties, and so he may hear your Supplications.

Yet, you don't know how to do it, even though you know that God has placed in your soul the solution that could save you. You were so blind you do not know how to raise yourself towards him, the Lord your God, who nonetheless is so close to you.

Learn to control your thoughts for at least a few seconds, the seconds of serenity you need to ascend to the heavenly light. God is within your reach. Dedicate yourself to it, entirely and exclusively, for a few minutes a day, every day. You can soon govern your thoughts at will, whatever the environment you are in, in the solitude of your room or in the hubbub of the city. You can make all your ideas converge for a duration that will seem to you close to infinity, but which will last only a few terrestrial minutes. With some experience, you'll be able to focus all your thoughts towards your goal and to elevate yourself towards the Lord. Doing an elevation will become for you as easy as turning on and off a light switch.

Now, try it by yourself! Pick biblical verses and spend twenty to thirty minutes on studying them. Read them again and again, until you understand each word and the apparent meaning of the text. Try to discover if there are other possible meanings that the biblical author could have hidden into it, intentionally or not.

During this activity, shut off your senses to external sensory stimulation. Set your sensory, visual, auditory, olfactory, physical perceptions, to sleeping mode, as if to isolate your mind in a hermetically sealed bubble. Make yourself deaf to any outside solicitation, the phone ringing, the cries of playing children, the scent of a good meal simmering on the stove, and so on. Actively repress any parasitic thought that crosses your mental space and prevents you from devoting yourself entirely to God—professional duties, health issues, an assignment you have not completed, etc.

The Bible says: "I sleep, but my heart waketh" (Sg 5:2). However, don't fall asleep! Keep your heart awake and stay alert to your environment. Remain conscious that you are reading Bible verses. Take advantage of the momentary respite offered by your victory over parasitic thoughts, and try to concentrate your liberated mind on the texts you have chosen, to better understand and assimilate them. It is useless at this stage to use the computational power of your brain to think.

Your mind is curiously made. When, while driving, the traffic light turns red, for instance, you unequivocally understand that you have to stop, and you need not think about it. In the same way, when your intellect is free from external solicitations and parasitic thoughts, it can solve problems with the lightness of a butterfly, and it finds solutions with no efforts.

Practice this exercise in many circumstances, at work, while shopping at the supermarket, while cooking or cleaning, while watching television, etc. Do not be disappointed if you can't do it on your first try. Try again as often as necessary. The more you practice, the easier it will be for you to turn on your internal switch to put your mind in a state of communication with the Lord.

You will quickly learn how you can gain a good mastery of your thought system. Your brain, a very flexible tool, will soon understand there are times when it must leave room for an activity vital to you. It will get accustomed to leaving you alone for a few moments, no more than a few moments, and all the energy will be at your disposal to help you reach that state of profound serenity you need. When a well-trained pet dog is walking next to his master, he knows that he must sit and wait quietly when his master meets another person and talk with him. A good dog will wait until the conversation is over before resuming his walk. The same goes for your intellect, which you can train like a pet.

Your mind is not your enemy; On the contrary, it could be your best friend. Like a faithful dog, it will do what you expect from it, but like with a good dog, you must compel it to some serious training.

As long as parasitic thoughts continue to interfere with your desire to focus on a single subject, keep training regularly and persistently. Do not despair, persevere!

Light bulbs emit particles of light called photons in all directions. This produces a halo of soft light in a limited space. The rays of light bulbs produce come from the same point and are dispersed widely by distancing themselves from one another. These rays are said to be divergent or incoherent. Lasers produce coherent rays, which photons do not split from one another. They remain parallel. This coherence gives laser beams a surprising power, energy, and reach. Lasers can send a lot of light to a small remote spot. You want your thoughts to do the same. No prayer can be efficient if it is not done in serenity. Eliminate stray thoughts and external noises; Domesticate divergent ideas, and force all your faculties and feelings to converge towards God, your unique goal.

When someone shakes your arm, and tells you, "Well, what were you thinking, didn't you hear that I asked you the same question three times?" Or: "a glass fell from my hands and broke on the kitchen tile floor. Didn't you hear, were you in the clouds?" And so, you may say to yourself, "yes, I was even higher than the clouds, and I intend to go back there often, for a very dear friend of mine lives there."

Ignore them and bear the consequences

When you are deeply imbued with the presence of God in your heart, it is this burning faith in his appearance that will save you and will prompt you to return to your inner sanctuary where he dwells and where you know you can find him.

When you access your inner sanctuary, you clearly see what's happening in you. You will see the disorder of your thoughts, and you will put them in order; you will review and evaluate your spirituality; you will also clean your mind and sweep away parasitic thoughts and unwanted noises, so you may finally hear God. Alone and shielded from sensory stimulation and solicitations from the outside world, you will be in ideal conditions to get nigh to God and create a strong personal relationship with him.

God's spirit that dwells in you gives you the incredible ability to achieve sanctification all by yourself, to elevate your soul towards God, and to achieve the purpose for which you have been created: fulfilling God's Will.

Self-effacement and Surrender

Self-effacement, followed by surrender to the Lord appearance, is the ultimate act of worship through self-sacrifice to the Lord. This does not differ from Abraham's sacrifice of his son Isaac, when, at God's request, Abraham, with no hesitation, raised his arm to immolate with his own hand his beloved son on the altar of God. He thus offered God the most handsome proof of unconditional faith that can be conceived.

The Scripture says, "I have set the Lord always before me: because he is at my right hand, I shall not be moved." (Ps 16:8). "My soul thirsteth for God, for the living God: when shall I come and appear before God?" (Ps 42:2).

More than simple submission, self-surrender is a state of extreme humility and abnegation that will lead you to a total abdication of your ego and even of your very own existence. The surrender into the hands of God of all that constitutes your ego includes your thoughts, your emotions, your desires, your will, your hopes, and your image. The effacement consists in substituting an egocentric life for a god-centric one, renouncing your own will for His Will, could be accomplished, like did Christ. "Father, if thou be willing, remove this cup from me: nevertheless not my will, but thine, be done." (Lk 22:42). And in doing so, you will also fulfill the divine precept, "Thou shalt be perfect with the Lord thy God." (Dt 18:13).

By renouncing your ego up to the very consciousness of your existence, you will transcend your temporal nature, and you will enter the spiritual kingdom. You will become a vector of the divine will within the divine work of creation. By effacement and surrender, you will be transported from where you are to where you ought to be. The offering of one's own self is the highest offering that man can make to the altar of God. The LORD said, "Ye shall seek me, and find me, when ye shall search for me with all your heart. And I will be found of you, saith the Lord." (Jer 29:13–14).

It is through Elevation, effacement, and surrender of your ego that you will encounter God who dwells in you. The Bible says: "The fining pot for silver, and the furnace for gold." (Prv 27:21). Like gold freed from its gangue of scoria by the fire of the furnace, and like silver refined by the fining-pot, the elevation frees the spirit that God has placed in you from the gangue of impurities you have let accumulate in your heart, to make it shine again.

During your spiritual elevation, you ought to be indifferent to all temporal things. Leave the past in oblivion and the future to providence and entrust to

the Lord the exclusiveness of the present moment that bears within the revelation of His Will.

The intensity of your commitment depends on your faculty of obliteration and abandonment to rely entirely on God and to rely on him for all your material and spiritual needs, says the the Bible. "Who against hope believed in hope" (Rom 4:18a).

This amounts to gradually substituting for your own will the will of God; To renounce all your natural inclinations, however positive they may be, leave only one valid option to your will—that of imitating God in all things.

The Bible says, "Draw nigh to God, and he will draw nigh to you. Cleanse your hands, ye sinners; and purify your hearts, ye double minded." (Jas 4: 8).

After you got rid of all traces of bonds with your ego of flesh and fulfilled the biblical recommendations, you will be ready to unite with the Divine Spirit, for flesh cannot mingle with the divine light. By thus distancing yourself from your physical body and from your thoughts, which are both of material nature, the sublimated man you will become, will be different, an ethereal, spiritual, seraphic nature, compatible with divine light. The divine in you attracted by the divine of heavens will merge with it, into the consecration of all your efforts at sanctification and elevation and your fulfillment of the biblical decree: "Thou shalt love the Lord thy God with all thine heart, and with all thy soul, and with all thy might." (Dt 6:5, 10:12, Mt 22:37, Mk 12:30, Lk 10:27).

The Divine Spirit, which God has placed in your heart, as in the heart of every man, aspires to meet the divine Spirit in heaven and merge with it. If you had not been created in the image of God, you could probably not find your model. You are an image of God, and God is your original model. Images always aspire to see their model, and they find peace only when they see it.

The Image of the Glory of God

After successfully accomplishing your elevation, you will learn of the divine presence. You will realize that all you had done before to be heard by the Lord was only a vain agitation, a comedy, but ineffective. The Lord said, "Forasmuch as this people draw near me with their mouth, and with their lips do honour me, but have removed their heart far from me, and their fear toward me is taught by the precept of men." (Is 29:13). In this verse, the expression "a precept of men" means a doctrine created by man, taught by man, and not inspired by the divine Word. This experience is unspeakable for the blessed ones who get to experience it at least once.

How will you know that you are in his presence? God has no physical traits or anthropomorphic forms. Do not expect to see a smiling character with a big white beard, like Santa Claus. This simple evocation is somewhat blasphemous, for you know that the Bible says: "Thou canst not see my face: for there shall no man see me, and live." (Ex 33:20).

The people who have lived through this beautiful experience don't know the impulse that causes witnesses of much more insignificant events to hasten to tell the media and their neighbors the extraordinary event they witnessed. Everyone may have his fifteen minutes of celebrity, isn't he?

Although each is unique, and the experience of one is not identical to the experience of others, the blessed ones who lived this incredible moment in the presence of God report they have felt an inner brightness, like the unprecedented brilliance of the theophany of Mount Sinai, when God's manifestation appears, accompanied by thunder and lightning; and the whole mountain smokes and quakes, and a voice reveals to Moses the Ten Commandments. They were filled with a feeling that resembled absolute happiness.

But what did they see? What did they witness? They felt

God, and they saw the image of the glory of the Lord. "In the morning, then ye shall see the glory of the Lord" (Ex 16:7a). It is by these words "The Glory of the Lord" that the Scriptures describe the appearance of God before mortals. The Bible says: "They looked towards the wilderness, and, behold, the glory of the Lord appeared in the cloud." (Ex 16:10b). "The sight of the glory of the Lord was like devouring fire on the top of the mount in the eyes of the children of Israel." (Ex 24:17). When Moses had built the tabernacle, God filled it with His presence. "Then a cloud covered the tent of the congregation, and the glory of the Lord filled the tabernacle." (Ex 40:34). Moses himself could not enter the tabernacle when the presence of God was dwelling in it. "Moses was not able to enter into the tent of the congregation, because the cloud abode thereon, and the glory of the Lord filled the tabernacle." (Ex 40:35).

At Moses's request, Aaron addressed the assembly of the children of Israel and asked them to make all the preparations for the great sacrifice of thanksgiving. "To day the Lord will appear unto you." (Lv 9: 4). Then Moses, in his turn, addressed the assembly, and, confirming that they would "see" God, he said to them, "This is the thing which the Lord commanded that ye should do: and the glory of the Lord shall appear unto you." (Lv 9:6). It is, therefore, by referring to the image of "the glory of God" that the biblical authors represented how God would appear before men since God cannot be seen by men.

After performing the sacrificial acts of thanksgiving, the prediction of Moses was fulfilled; The Bible says, "And Moses and Aaron went into the tabernacle of the congregation, and came out, and blessed the people: and the glory of the Lord appeared unto all the people." (Lv 9:23).

Moses had brought forth his people out of Egypt, and then they wandered in the wilderness in search of Canaan, the land that God had promised them. After a few years of wandering, they lost confidence in their god and in their leaders, Moses and Aaron. God, irritated by the lack of faith of the children of Israel, suggested that Moses send a group of scouts from one tribe of Israel to explore the desert and find the land God had given them promised and the best way to achieve it. The people accepted this proposition, and Moses had it approved by God. God acceded to their request immediately, but he intended to punish them. When they were back, the scouts said that the lands they had explored were not habitable and that their inhabitants were ferocious and powerful. They urged the people to dismiss Moses and to choose another leader. "And the glory of the Lord appeared in the tabernacle of the congregation before all the children of Israel." (Nm 14:10, 16:19, 16:42, 20:6).

When Solomon inaugurated the temple of Jerusalem, which he had designed with his father, King David, it was the occasion for great ceremonies and sacrifices to consecrate the temple to the Lord God of Israel. The Bible says, "The glory of the Lord had filled the house of the Lord." (1 Kgs 8:11; 2 Chr 5:14, 7:1,2).

Isaiah promised those who walked in the way of God that God would always be with them. The Bible says, "The glory of the Lord shall be thy reward." (Is 58: 8); And, "Arise, shine; for thy light is come, and the glory of the Lord is risen upon thee." (Is 60: 1).

Ezekiel was a great prophet. God communicated with him through dreams that he knew how to interpret brilliantly. Thanks to the power of his prophecy, Ezekiel could see what was happening in Jerusalem while still in his 25th year of exile in Babylon.

The narrative of Ezekiel 8 says that he could see his people had deviated from the laws and started practicing pagan rites. He also witnessed the glory of God leaving the temple. The Scripture says, "Then the glory of the Lord went up from the cherub and stood over the threshold of the house, and the house was filled with the cloud, and the court was full of the brightness of the Lord's glory." (Ez 10:4); And "The glory of the Lord departed from off the threshold of the house, and stood over the cherubims." (Ez 10:18); And again, "The glory of the Lord went up from the midst of the city, and stood upon the mountain which is on the east side of the city." (Ez 11:23).

He saw, at last, the destruction of the temple, which had taken place fourteen years before. But one day, Ezekiel had a beautiful dream. He was taken to Jerusalem, where he visited the new temple, which the Lord wished to see rebuilt. This temple existed only in his dream, but this dream was so real that Ezekiel could not only visit it but also take its exact measurements. The accuracy of these measures, as revealed in the Scriptures, has been verified by today's architects.

Ezekiel saw the divine presence as an image of the glory of God surrounded by a bright rainbow light. The Scripture says, "As the appearance of the bow that is in the cloud in the day of rain, so was the appearance of the brightness round about. This was the appearance of the likeness of the glory of the Lord. And when I saw it, I fell upon my face, and I heard a voice of one that spake." (Ez 1:28). Ezekiel felt God several times. The Scripture says, "Then I arose, and went forth into the plain: and, behold, the glory of the Lord stood there, as the glory which I saw by the river of Chebar: and I fell on my face." (Ez 3:23). He saw the glory of God coming forward to take possession of his dwelling, the new temple of Jerusalem. The Scripture says, "And, behold, the glory of the God of Israel came from the way of the east: and his voice was like a noise of many waters: and the earth shined with his glory." (Ez 43:2).

Then he saw the glory of God entering the temple: "And the glory of the Lord came into the house" (Ez 43:4a). He then felt that

God filled the temple: "The glory of the Lord filled the house." (Ez 43: 5; 44: 4). This vision confirms the prophecy of Haggai, who had predicted that God would fill the new temple with his presence. Scripture says, "I will fill this house with glory, saith the Lord of hosts." (Hg 2:7b).

> **When you are higher, but not yet at the top of your Jacob's ladder, you will be grabbed and taken away. You will no longer know being or having been. You will no longer feel the need to speak, nor to question yourself, nor even to think. Your Supplication will be silent, and God will infuse in you his immanent love, which has the taste of perfect happiness. You will have the feeling that you are living in eternity, and that's what it's all about, for, during these few earthly seconds that you'll spend in God's presence, you'll be experiencing eternity.**

Everything comprises multiple facets. Today, you see only one of the many aspects of things. Invisible things remain hidden to all your senses. One day, however, in your eternal life, all things, whether they had been visible or hidden to your eyes, you'll see them in their entirety, in the light of the Spirit. Then you'll understand everything, and you will know everything. Nothing will remain hidden to you.

How to Know God Is Talking to You?

In his late years, the high priest Eli took the young shepherd Samuel to his service, to teach him the Law. Eli and Samuel both lived in the temple of Jerusalem, where Eli officiated. One night, when Samuel had just fallen asleep, he thought he heard a voice

Ignore them and bear the consequences

calling him by name. Samuel ran to Eli's bedside, but the latter said to him, "I have not called you." Samuel went back to his bed. Again, Samuel heard a voice calling him. He rushed to Eli, but Eli made the same answer yet, "I have not called you." Three times Samuel heard that voice calling him, but each time, he received the same response from Eli: "I have not called you." Then Eli understood that the Lord called Samuel, and he said to the boy, "If you hear a voice calling you, again, answer this: 'Speak, Lord; for thy servant heareth.'" (1 Sm 3:9). Samuel went back to bed, and when he heard the voice call him again, he responded, "Speak; for thy servant heareth." (1 Sm 3:10)

To this day, Samuel had never conversed with God and had never been in His presence. Thus, he could not recognize the voice of God when he called him by his name (1 Sm 3:1–10). His spiritual development had not yet been achieved, considering his young age, and his intuition was still in formation. He owed to Eli's wisdom this conversation he had with the Lord that day.

This call was imperative to Samuel. In this first conversation, the Lord announced to him the imminent death of his master, the prophet Eli, but, more important, God revealed that he chose him, Samuel, the young shepherd, to succeed Eli as God's prophet.

I hope you will not be away from your phone the day you receive such a call, and above all, I hope you will recognize the voice of the Lord when he calls you. Are you sure that you'll know who's calling? Are you sure you'll recognize his voice? How can you be so sure? If I told you that God does not communicate with a man by voice, and does not use the words of human languages to communicate with them, would you still be so sure?

The Language of God

How does God address humans? How does he communicate with them? Does the lord shake the earth with his powerful baritone voice? Does he appear in visions or in dreams? Does he transmit his will through his angels who visit men during their sleep?

The Scriptures speak with every generation, with the power of divine authority and the incredible beauty of revealed truths. No literary work derived from the talent of man possesses such qualities. Inspiration in the Bible differs from the inspiration that allows great writers, poets, and artists to produce literary and artistic masterpieces. Today's reader is so touched by the wisdom and truth that the Scriptures reveal that the emotion he feels deep within his being is comparable to that felt by the patriarchs and the prophets the first time they realized that they were inspired by the Lord's Spirit.

The immutability of the Word of God is the result of the immutability of God, so his word is never and will never be obsolete. But this is especially evidence that what God said in ancient times to the patriarchs and biblical prophets is still true today, and will remain true forever. Therefore, whoever wants to know the Word of God must read and reread the Scriptures, for he will find the answers he seeks before seeking higher. It is, therefore, right to say that the first word you will hear from God will come to you through the Scripture.

The sacred writers of the Bible, inspired by the Spirit of God, transcribed the divine revelation into human language with high precision and fidelity. These authors were humans who, being inspired by God, wrote what God had commanded them to write. The Bible says: "Thus speaketh the Lord God of Israel, saying, write thee all the words that I have spoken unto thee in a book." (Jer 30:2). As for Moses, "Moses wrote all the words of the Lord." (Ex 24:4). The words they used and the principles they transcribed were God-inspired. Not a single word or precept came from their own mind.

The Bible says, "I certify you, brethren, that the gospel which was preached of me is not after man. For I neither received it of man, neither was I taught it, but by the revelation of Jesus Christ." (Gal 1:11–12); And again: "When ye received the word of God which ye heard of us, ye received it not as the word of men, but as it is in truth, the word of God, which effectually worketh also in you that believe." (1 Thes 2:13b, c). However, the style of their writing is the personal style of the authors. Their style is sometimes strongly marked by their personality, their culture, and their profession. Thus, Matthew, who was a tax collector, was particularly marked by a scene, which, moreover, he is the only one to have reported. This scene took place at Capernaum, where Jesus and Peter were asked to pay a fee: 'When they came to Capernaum, those who perceived the two drachmas addressed Peter, and said to him, "Isn't your master paying the two drachmas? He saith, Yes. And when he was come into the house, Jesus prevented him, saying, what thinkest thou, Simon? of whom do the kings of the earth take custom or tribute? of their own children, or of strangers? Peter saith unto him, of strangers. Jesus saith unto him, then are the children free." (Mt 17:24-26).

Similarly, Luke, who practiced medicine, is the only one to have reported, in the parable of the Good Samaritan, an event in which the Samaritan gives a victim of aggression medical care worthy of a man of the art, says the Bible. "And Jesus answering said, A certain man went down from Jerusalem to Jericho, and fell among thieves, which stripped him of his raiment, and wounded him, and departed, leaving him half dead." (Lk 10:30). Luke, with his medical knowledge, describes the care of the injured person, as he himself would have applied them in the exercise of his profession. "But a certain Samaritan, as he journeyed, came where he was: and when he saw him, he had compassion on him, and went to him, and bound up his wounds, pouring in oil and wine, and set him on his own beast, and brought him to an inn, and took care of him." (Lk 10:33–34). As a man of science, Luke says that his writings were not done lightly; they resulted from careful research. "It seemed good to me also, having had perfect understanding of all things from the very first, to write unto thee in order" (Lk 1:3).

Despite these inevitable human influences, it can be stated that no human will or idea has interfered with the Divine Word. The biblical writers did not write on their own initiative; they merely transcribed, for posterity, the word of God imbued in them by the divine Spirit. The Bible says, "All scripture is given by inspiration of God" (2 Tm 3:16a). And: "The prophecy came not in old time by the will of man: but holy men of God spake as they were moved by the Holy Ghost." (2 Pt 1:21). It should be noted, however, that if this is true for the original language used by the sacred authors, the same is not true of the translations of the Bible, which are human works, therefore subject to fallibility.

How Did God Speak to the Prophets?

Let's walk through the Bible, and discover how the prophets talked about their own personal experiences, how God spoke to them, how they received God's Word, how they were assured that their speeches were not the product of their own mind, but instead, they were inspired by God. The patriarchs, the prophets, and the apostles revealed that they were filled with the Spirit of God and spoke what the Lord had put in their mouths.

Jeremiah said: "The Lord said unto me, behold, I have put my words in thy mouth." (Jer 1:9). David took no personal credit for what he taught, and to explain how a modest shepherd could come to prophesy as he did, he said, "The Spirit of the Lord spake by me, and his word was in my tongue." (2 Sm 23:2).

When the biblical prophets were called by the Lord to prophesize, God filled them with his spirit, and they became inspired, so although they were speaking with their own mouths and their own words, what they were saying was the inspired Word of God. The Scripture says, "I have filled him with the Spirit of God, with wisdom, with understanding, and with knowledge for all kinds of works" (Ex 31:3; 35:31). We can deduct that they did probably not hear a voice they recognized as being God's voice, but instead, the prophets understood God had filled them with his Spirit, and therefore, when speaking, they were merely voicing God's Word.

It even came to pass that the LORD put his words in the mouth of an animal, Balaam's donkey, so exasperated he was by the want of understanding of Balaam. The Bible says. "And the Lord opened the mouth of the ass, and it said unto Balaam, what have I done unto thee, that thou hast smitten me these three times?" (Nm 22:28).

Ezekiel describes in great detail his experience, his encounter with God, and how the Lord spoke to him through the Spirit and through divine inspiration, says the Bible. "The heavens were opened, and I saw visions of God." (Ez 1:1). Then Ezekiel saw an image of the Glory of the Lord a representation of the presence of God. The Bible says, "I saw as the colour of amber, as the appearance of fire round about within it, from the appearance of his loins even upward, and from the appearance of his loins even downward, I saw as it were the appearance of fire, and it had brightness round about. As the appearance of the bow that is in the cloud in the day of rain, so was the appearance of the brightness round about. This was the appearance of the likeness of the glory of the Lord. And when I saw it, I fell upon my face, and I heard a voice of one that spake." (Ez 1:27–28). Ezekiel goes on: "He said unto me, Son of man, stand upon thy feet, and I will speak unto thee. And the spirit entered into me when he spake unto me, and set me upon my feet, that I heard him that spake unto me." (Ez 2:1–2). Ezekiel lived the same experience several times. The Bible says, "Then the spirit entered into me, and set me upon my feet, and spake with me, and said unto me, go, shut thyself within thine house." (Ez 3:24). Ezekiel's testimony is like those of the other great prophets of the Bible.

The Lord spoke to Joel. The Bible says, "The word of the Lord that came to Joel" (Jl 1:1). Filled with the Spirit of God, Joel predicted that all men would be filled with the Spirit of God and that they could also prophesy through inspiration. The Bible says, "I will pour out my spirit upon all flesh; and your sons and your daughters shall prophesy, your old men shall dream dreams, your young men shall see visions: And also upon the servants and upon the handmaids in those days will I pour out my spirit." (Jl 2:28–29). Then Joel revealed God's promise. The Scripture says, "Whosoever shall call on the name of the Lord shall be delivered" (Jl 2:32).

Daniel was also filled with the Spirit of God and inspired. It is said in the Bible that King Belshazzar, the son, and successor of Nebuchadnezzar, said: "I have even heard of thee, that the spirit of the gods is in thee, and that light and understanding and excellent wisdom is found in thee." (Dn 5:14). Daniel had just interpreted for King Belshazzar, a dream that meant that the Lord had put an end to his reign. The same evening Belshazzar died. Thanks to the divine inspiration that guided him, King Nebuchadnezzar had been very appreciative of Daniel's talents at prophecy, as he often relied on Daniel to point out to him the right interpretation of a dream. Once, Daniel revealed to him not only the vision that the king had forgotten, but he also gave him the correct interpretation of that dream.

Joseph had been sold as a slave by his own brothers jealous of him. He survived years of the ill-treatment he received in the prisons of Egypt and as a captive. However, Joseph had been filled with the Spirit of God. Like Daniel, he interpreted a strange dream that Pharaoh had, and that his magicians could not explain.

The Bible says, "Pharaoh said unto his servants, can we find such a one as this is, a man in whom the Spirit of God is?" (Gn 41:38).

Since he was anointed by Samuel, David was filled with the Spirit of God. The Scripture says: "Samuel took the horn of oil, and anointed him in the midst of his brethren: and the Spirit of the Lord came upon David from that day forward." (1 Sm 16:13).

David was inspired by the Spirit of God with which he had been filled. By divine inspiration, he wrote and put the psalms to music to the glory of God. The Bible says, "I will incline mine ear to a parable: I will open my dark saying upon the harp." (Ps 49: 4), which means, "I will listen very carefully to a metaphor, and my harp will help me unleash its hidden meaning."

David knew how to calm Saul when he was moved by evil thoughts. The Bible says, "When the evil spirit from God was upon Saul that David took a harp, and played with his hand: so Saul was refreshed, and was well, and the evil spirit departed from him." (1 Sm 16:23).

Paul explained how he prophesied and preached the Good Word during his many journeys to remote and sometimes hostile lands. Paul thought that if he could carry out such missions and preach the Gospel of Christ in every place he visited, even the more hostiles to him, it was thanks to the power of the Divine Spirit. The Bible says. "Through mighty signs and wonders, by the power of the Spirit of God; so that from Jerusalem, and round about unto Illyricum, I have fully preached the gospel of Christ." (Rom 15:19). "We have received, not the spirit of the world, but the spirit which is of God; that we might know the things that are freely given to us of God." (1 Cor 2:12).

How God Speaks to Man Nowadays

The Bible says: "For God speaketh once, yea twice, yet man perceiveth it not" (Jb 33:14). So God speaks to men, however, sometimes in one way, sometimes in another, and men are not conscious that God is talking to them. This verse reveals two truths. The first is that God uses plenty of different means to speak with humans, so numerous and so diverse, that man could not understand them had he been told about it. The second truth in this verse is that these men to whom God spoke remember the Divine Message correctly, but they do not always remember the form this "conversation" took. The Divine Word is inscribed in the mind of men so powerfully that it conceals how it was delivered, although no doubt as to its authenticity can subsist. This is what the end of the verse means "man perceiveth it not" (Jb 33:14); that is: "men are not conscious that God is talking to them."

How to interpret "Word" in the expression "Word of God"? One cannot take this word in its literal sense, for it would implicitly assume that God has an anthropomorphic form, a human shape; It would also imply that God has anthropopathic qualities, and would, therefore, be subject to the same appetites and desires as a man, and would feel the same feelings as humans.

God is infinite, and the infinite cannot be contained in any container, such as a body that is finite. If we did not admit this principle, then we would have to acknowledge that God is made of matter, which would be contrary to the image of a God-Spirit, which befits the enlightened believer. God cannot be clothed in

Ignore them and bear the consequences

characteristics peculiar to man, for this would lead to a more material rendition of God, and therefore less divine, which would only be heresy and pure idolatry.

How can we interpret the expression "Word of God" if we rid it of all anthropopathic intent? If this seems to you hard to understand, remember Job's advice: "Ask now the beasts, and they shall teach thee; and the fowls of the air, and they shall tell thee: Or speak to the earth, and it shall teach thee: and the fishes of the sea shall declare unto thee." (Jb 12:7–8).

So, let's ask the bee. Bees "speak" to each other. The oldest and most experienced bees of a hive are explorers. They continuously travel around the colony or swarm in search of new sources of nectar. They sometimes travel several kilometers to find the best food sources. Upon their return, they transmit the information they have collected to the gatherers of nectar and pollen. They use a sort of complex dance language well known today, thanks to the work of the Austrian ethologist Karl von Frisch. A scout bee can communicate accurate information to gatherer brethren, as for instance, how far is the source of nectar they discovered; The position of this source regarding an angle formed, on the one hand, by the direction of the sun, and that of the newly discovered source. The explorer can also alert and warn the gatherers of dangers they faced during their searches, such as foreign bees from hostile colonies or predators. Thanks to the precision of their language, bees can also relay information on the quality of the sources of nectar they have discovered. Even more amazingly, ethologists, the researchers studying animal behavior, have found that bees can have democratic debates when, for instance, the colony becomes too large, and a group proclaims its independence to form a new swarm. Bees are said to "speak." They use a language that does not resemble human tongues but a language specific to their species, and that allows them to communicate with as much precision as human words allow. When God speaks to men, He uses the language He deems the most appropriate for the circumstances. God wants that you understand his message and act according to His Will. To him, it does not matter if you identify the "language" he will use to speak to you.

God does not use these words so useful to men to communicate. Though it must be admitted, the words of human languages are limited as to the variety and precision of the concepts which they are supposed to convey. Professional translators know of this when they cannot translate a simple text from one language into another, and sometimes they have to make an approximation. Some poems are, for example, impossible to render in another language, for the nuances and emotions they contain in their original vernacular are lost in translation.

When the Bible says that God "speaks," it is a metaphor, an imaged way of expressing an idea or a concept more adequately. Since words of human languages are quite restricted, images may convey more meaning than words, and the adage "A picture is worth a thousand words," is proven to be true.

The Bible reveals many instances of direct conversations between God and the patriarchs. The most memorable of these conversations is that which God had with Moses at Mount Horeb, where God gave Moses his commandments to serve as written law for the people of Israel and for all future generations.

These conversations between God and Moses were clear and precise, so Moses could transcribe and transmit them to the people whose destiny God had entrusted to him. But how was this conversation going? In what language? Only Moses himself could say. But we can easily imagine that Moses would have made the same answer as Job, who said, "Man perceiveth it not" (Jb 33:14).

Ignore them and bear the consequences

When Mary and Aaron manifested some resentment towards Moses, who had married an Ethiopian girl, God heard them say, "Hath the Lord indeed spoken only by Moses? hath he not spoken also by us? And the Lord heard it." (Nm 12:2). Then the Lord said to Mary and Aaron, "Hear now my words: If there be a prophet among you, I the Lord will make myself known unto him in a vision, and will speak unto him in a dream." (Nm 12: 6). Therefore, it is thus that God interacts with prophets. He appears to them in a vision and speaks to them in a dream. In the Bible, the prophet Joel confirms, "In the last days, saith God, I will pour out of my Spirit upon all flesh: and your sons and your daughters shall prophesy, and your young men shall see visions, and your old men shall dream dreams: and on my servants and on my handmaidens, I will pour out in those days of my Spirit; and they shall prophesy" (Acts 2:17–18). The Scripture further confirms: "For God speaketh once, yea twice, yet man perceiveth it not. In a dream, in a vision of the night, when deep sleep falleth upon men, in slumberings upon the bed; Then he openeth the ears of men." (Jb 33:15).

It was also in a dream that God appeared to Jacob, and God spoke to him through a vision. "And he dreamed, and behold a ladder set up on the earth, and the top of it reached to heaven: and behold the angels of God ascending and descending on it." (Gn 28:12). This dream, in which this metaphorical image appears, was so easy to understand that Jacob felt no need to resort to the service of a dream interpreter, as there were plenty of them. Jacob had no doubt that God himself had "spoken" to him, to tell him he had to speak with him and create a strong and lasting relationship with him, for God had great plans for him. But what to think of the angels who appeared in the divine message in high numbers, ascending to God, others descending from the sky to go to Jacob? These angels represent another metaphorical image.

The angels climbing to the sky express the questions, anxieties, doubts, and demands that Jacob would address to God to receive the help he needed to carry out the critical mission that God intended to entrust to him; The angels who descend the ladder to go to him represent the messages that God would send to Jacob. This conversation, once initiated, would be permanent. This image is worth a thousand words, isn't it? But, could you say to yourself, how could Jacob be so sure of that? He could have understood, for instance, that all the angels on the ladder represented children in a playground playing speed races on a ladder. This dream could have been but another of those many nonsensical dreams we forget as soon as we open the eyes. No, this is impossible, for he who receives the word of God has no doubt about the message and its origin.

The attitude of Jacob, when he gets the Divine message, is straightforward. He is convinced without the shadow of a doubt that God has spoken to him, and he instantly understands the nature of the communication and what God wants him to do.

He, to whom God speaks in this way, understands. Why and how are you entitled to ask? Jacob was a sage from a prestigious lineage of patriarchs, Isaac, his father, and Abraham, his grandfather. His prestigious ancestors taught him to listen to his intuitions. If you do not have the chance to have parents that are patriarchs or prophets, you will know how to interpret a divine message. But would you be able to recognize the voice of God? Are you sufficiently attentive to your intuitions to understand that the Lord is calling you?

Often, those who believe that they have heard God speak to them and do not understand what God has told them, and those who ask themselves whether God spoke to them, alas, they have heard nothing. They have simply had an ordinary dream, or at worst, they have been victims of hallucinations. It is useless for them to consult a psychic or any other professional charlatan. The latter will not know more than they do, but they will know how to make their wallets lighter. The Bible says. "The prophet that hath a dream, let him tell a dream; and he that hath my word, let him speak my word faithfully. What is the chaff to the wheat? saith the Lord." (Jer 23:28).

After he had berated Mary and Aaron, the Lord explained to them what kind of relationship he had with Moses and how he spoke with him. The Lord said, "My servant Moses is not so, who is faithful in all mine house. With him will I speak mouth to mouth, even apparently, and not in dark speeches; and the similitude of the Lord shall he behold: wherefore then were ye not afraid to speak against my servant Moses?" (Nm 12:7–8).

In these verses, the Lord reveals that his relationship with Moses is unique and different from all relations that he has with anyone else. However, God also reveals that even Moses cannot see him, for a while he reveals himself to Moses with no mystery, Moses can only see an image of the presence of the Lord, which Ezekiel calls "An image of the glory of The Lord" (Ez 1:28). It is an unheard-of privilege, but must we not see in this, a divine confirmation that God has no anthropomorphic forms; That nothing can contain him; That it is therefore not made of flesh; And, that his speech cannot be made of words.

God speaks to men by means which exceed sensory perception, which in man is limited to the five senses. He speaks to them through the Spirit, through their consciousness and subconsciousness, by depositing in their mind the message which he wishes to transmit to them, in dreams, images, ideas, or irresistible impulses, or by merely whispering to them the decision they should take. The Bible says. "Know ye not that ye are the temple of God, and that the Spirit of God dwelleth in you?" (1 Cor 3:16).

When, on awakening, you forget a dream that impressed

you, it does not necessarily mean this dream was not the bearer of a divine message. Do not be sorry to have forgotten so quickly. Maybe God simply put his word in your subconscious, which positively influences your intuition and your inspiration.

King Nebuchadnezzar was very disturbed by a dream he had during his sleep, and that he forgot in the early morning. He immediately summoned the magicians, the astrologers, and all the enchanters of the kingdom and gave them instruction. "I have dreamed a dream, and my spirit was troubled to know the dream." (Dn 2:3). The magicians answered, "Tell thy servants the dream, and we will shew the interpretation." (Dn 2:4). Before the dubious air of the magicians, the king added, "If ye will not make known unto me the dream, with the interpretation thereof, ye shall be cut in pieces, and your houses shall be made a dunghill." (Dn 2:5). The magicians, frightened, replied to the king: "There is none other that can shew it before the king, except the gods, whose dwelling is not with flesh." (Dn 2:11). Then the king became angry and commanded that all the wise men of Babylon should be destroyed. The prophet Daniel, understanding he was in danger of suffering the same fate, went to the king and begged him to give him time to provide the king with an explanation. In a nocturnal vision, the secret was revealed to Daniel. He went again to the king, and spoke with him. "The secret which the king hath demanded cannot the wise men, the astrologers, the magicians, the soothsayers, shew unto the king; But there is a God in heaven that revealeth secrets, and maketh known to the king Nebuchadnezzar what shall be in the latter days. Thy dream, and the visions of thy head upon thy bed, are these" (Dn 2:27–28).

To the astonishment of the king, Daniel reminded him in detail of the complex dream he had had, and that had so disturbed him and which he could no longer remember. Then Daniel interpreted for the king the message that this dream carried. In his message,

Ignore them and bear the consequences

God revealed to the king what would be his destiny and that of his successors. When he had finished his interpretation, he added: "The dream is true, and its explanation is certain." (Dn 2:45). Then the king, acknowledging the superiority and omnipotence of the god of Israel, fell on his face and bowed before Daniel, saying, "The king answered unto Daniel, and said, of a truth it is, that your God is a God of gods, and a lord of kings, and a revealer of secrets, seeing thou couldest reveal this secret." (Dn 2:47).

You might ask yourself if the events announced in the dream would have taken place if Daniel had not reminded the king of the vision and given his interpretation and if this dream had been forgotten without hope of return. The answer is yes! All the predicted events would have happened, but one can imagine that King Nebuchadnezzar, having not been able to remember the dream, and therefore, unable to interpret the divine message, his destiny would have been changed.

Listening to God

Intuition will alert you, and inspiration will enlighten you. Guided by intuition and enlightenment, you will accomplish what God asks you to accomplish. These two qualities are delicate dispositions of the mind, independent of intelligence. A person may have an average intellect while being very receptive to intuition and inspiration. They are comparable to wisdom, but, while the latter is mainly based on endogenous sources, intuition listens to exogenous sources. Inspiration feeds on data that come from all possible sources.

The Bible reveals that when Abraham was preparing to sacrifice his son Isaac to obey the Lord's request, an angel of God intervened to stop his gesture: "Lay not thine hand upon the lad, neither do thou anything unto him: for now I know that thou fearest God, seeing thou hast not withheld thy son, thine only son from me." (Gn 22:12).

Thanks to his intuition, Abraham recognized the voice of God, and he obeyed with great relief and sincere gratitude. His inspiration pushed him to look around had God placed within his grasp an element that would allow him to conform to both the contradictory messages of the Lord: "Take now thy son, thine only son Isaac, whom thou lovest, and get thee into the land of Moriah; and offer him there for a burnt offering" (Gn 22:2), on the one hand, and "Lay not thine hand upon the lad, neither do thou anything unto him" (Gn 22:12). He did not know what he was looking for, but he obeyed his inspiration. Abraham was a man of great piety, naturally disposed to interpret his intuitions and to converse with God. He certainly knew that God would not only dictate his will, but would also give him the means to satisfy his profound and legitimate scruples. Abraham had to ask himself inwardly: "God first ordered me to sacrifice my son, and I will not do it, even if it is at his express request that I will not obey his initial request. This creates a doubt in me. I will always live with the consciousness of having breached a commandment from God. What to do?" Abraham then had an inspiration that whispered to him that God has probably foreseen a substitute solution. That happened. The Bible says. "Abraham lifted up his eyes, and looked, and behold behind him a ram caught in a thicket by his horns: and Abraham went and took the ram, and offered him up for a burnt offering in the stead of his son." (Gn 22:13). Need I say more?

The Bible abounds in similar examples. Have you read it? Have you studied it enough? All the answers to the questions you ask yourself or that you might ask are there. The Scriptures are the most significant source of inspiration. Does not your intuition tell you you should read it and reread it?

Ignore them and bear the consequences

To see and recognize an angel of God who carries a message from God, the recipient of the message must be receptive. The angel does not exist absent a responsive recipient if there is not an intuitive and inspired soul able to receive the Word of God.

The atmosphere is continuously crisscrossed by radio waves broadcast by thousands of radio stations around the world, but if you do not have a radio set to the right frequency and able to receive these signals and decode them, you will not hear the music of your favorite group.

Moses is the Patriarch who maintained perfect relations with God. The Lord said of Moses, "With him will I speak mouth to mouth, even apparently, and not in dark speeches; and the similitude of the Lord shall he behold: wherefore then were ye not afraid to speak against my servant Moses?" (Nm 12:8). This verse reveals that God spoke to Moses face-to-face without the help of an angel. His word was not based on metaphors, for God knew well that Moses understood him without ambiguity.

Moses could see an image of the presence of the Lord when he spoke to him. He saw the representation of the Glory of God. No other patriarch had ever had the same privileges. In the Bible, most patriarchs and prophets were generally visited in a dream by an angel carrying the Word of God.

I remember a little girl who liked to play the school teacher. She showed her friends a pious image depicting the idyllic scene of a blue-eyed angel wearing long curly golden hair that went down to his waist. He extended a protective hand over the head of two children playing too close to a torrent.

The little girl asked her young students sitting quietly in front of her, why does the angel have long hair? No one found the answer to this question, including me, I must admit. Then, after keeping them guessing to the end to show off her own erudition, she gave them the right answer: Angels have long hair because there are no barbers in paradise!

I still have a good laugh when I recall this story. Children's common sense is impressive, but it must lead us to reflect on the things that seem obvious to us. The Bible warns us against the pictorial representation of the divine reality, for these images, derived from the imagination of men, divert us from God.

In the Bible, these images are called idols; whether drawn on paper or carved in stone, these idols distract the believer from the one true God. The Bible says. "Thou shalt not make unto thee any graven image, or any likeness of anything that is in heaven above, or that is in the earth beneath, or that is in the water under the earth." (Ex 20:4).

God alone is worthy of worship. Idols, even those whose appearance is the most innocent, turn away from God the glory and adoration that only God deserves.

The Bible says: "The idols of the heathen are silver and gold, the work of men's hands. They have mouths, but they speak not; eyes have they, but they see not; They have ears, but they hear not; neither is there any breath in their mouths. They that make them are like unto them: so is every one that trusteth in them." (Ps 135:15–18).

Too many people still imagine the angels as graceful beings with a blue-eyed child's face, with long golden hair, and wearing a pair of large bird's wings. The young people of today would instead imagine angels like androids out of Star Wars. If this is your case, know that it is purely and only idol worshiping. The Bible says: "They that observe lying vanities forsake their own mercy." (Jon 2:8).

If you are receptive to the word of God and you receive a divine message, you will undoubtedly remember the message, but you will forget how it was delivered to you. An angel had carried it, but you did not see him. The Bible says: "How precious also are thy thoughts unto me, O God! how great is the sum of them!" (Ps 139: 17).

God's thoughts are impenetrable to man; And Paul confirms: "O the depth of the riches both of the wisdom and knowledge of God! how unsearchable are his judgments, and his ways past finding out!" (Rom 11:33). God's judgments are unfathomable, and His ways are incomprehensible to men.

Why don't we see God's messenger? There are two answers to this question. The first thing that comes to mind is that we are neither patriarch nor prophet. If he wants you to be His prophet, he will tell you plainly.

The other most crucial answer is revealed in the Scriptures. The Bible says, "He [the Lord] said, thou canst not see my face: for there shall no man see me, and live." (Ex 33:20).

Angels are emanations of God. No human can claim he saw God and continue to live. Moses himself did not see God, although God had allowed him to see an image of his presence. God and His Word are not severable, and seeing an angel means to perceive the Word of God and to see God.

How would God address you? You, who are neither a patriarch nor a prophet, but merely an honest and faithful believer whose essential desire to understand what God's Will means and consecrate your life to its fulfillment? This question is legitimate.

When rid of superstitious images and false representations of God, you will be ready to receive the Word of God and to be imbued of it, and you will no longer materially need to understand how his word has been conveyed to you.

Law #7
The Law of Consequences

"They cried, but there was none to save them: even unto the Lord, but he answered them not." (Ps 18:41)

What Does Consequence Mean?

Too many people still believe that devotion and worship consist primarily in practicing strict rites, whose choreography was written by their church. This includes: observing the divine commandments, abiding by the rules of ethical conduct, saying daily prayers and pre-written devotions, and showing up at church on Sundays. These believers, no one can deny that they are true believers, are convinced that they are in good standing with God, just because they have learned and can recite by heart those rules, rituals, prayers, and devotions that can be purchased at any good Christian bookstore. They are wrong!

Genuine devotions are not based on rules or rituals. They are made of personal will, of constant questioning, and of frequent references to the Scripture, the inspired Word of God. And, require that some essential moral qualities be developed, such as sincerity, honesty, and humility.

Consequences result from an action, and the latter produces effects. These consequences, whether they are direct or indirect, positive or negative, good or bad, result from the deed that generated them.

No action or category thereof is intrinsically good or bad a priori. Actions are judged only on their intentions and on their consequences. The reasons, whether conscious or unconscious, for a particular course of action, reveal, a priori, whether a deed is well or ill-intentioned.

The effects of an act will determine, afterward, whether this action was right or wrong. For most of life's choices, you can easily predict whether such a decision is likely to produce good or bad consequences because it's a matter of common sense. You may also have experienced similar situations. Isn't it true that wisdom is the art of foreseeing the legitimate consequences of established principles? Aren't you the sum of all the choices you made since your birth?

The more an action is in conformity with the Divine Will, the better the consequences. If a deed is likely to improve the well-being of many people, perhaps this deed is good. An action that produces prosperity to benefit its sole author is a selfish act, therefore not in conformity with the divine will. Though it is not necessarily bad, it does not qualify as being good.

Some actions can have severe consequences for you, but also for others. You may need to think twice before you make the right decision, and you may not find a satisfactory answer in your past personal experience. God will help you if you ask him.

The Scripture, the inspired Word of God, contains the answers to all your questions.

How can you make sure that your choices and deeds are conforming to God's will? Before you decide, ask yourself these questions on the direct and indirect consequences of the decisions you are about to take. This will allow you to evaluate if your choice might cause one of the following effects:

1. Could it cause harm to others?
2. Could it be harmful to God's Creation?
3. Am I going to break a holy commandment?
4. Am I unknowingly going to infringe on God's reserved domain?
5. Will it contribute to sustaining the Divine Creation?
6. Will it improve your well-being, your prosperity, or your health?
7. More importantly, will it also improve the well-being, prosperity or wealth of others?
8. Could your decision produce more benefits to others than to yourself?
9. Or, is it likely to produce beneficial effects not only for yourself but also for others?
10. Is your decision prone to help the needy?
11. Or is it inclined to help someone to get through life?
12. Is your choice meant to improve your spirituality?
13. Do you think it might enhance the image that God has of you?
14. Is it likely to develop your relationships with others?
15. Is this deed likely to strengthen your personal relationship with God?
16. Or, does it have the potential to improve your image of yourself?
17. Will it amplify your wisdom?
18. Can it produce beneficial consequences for people in general?
19. Are you sure you are doing what God wants you to do?
20. Is your deed going to make of you an idolater?

If you are mindful of the consequences inherent in your choices,

Ignore them and bear the consequences

you will behold the many effects that your actions may have on yourself and on others. Sequels may be harmful or favorable, direct or indirect, immediate, or asynchronous. Consequences must not be confused with retribution or punishment. This word sometimes sounds like a punishment inflicted on the perpetrator of a fault. That is not the case here. God created good, and he created evil, so he does not punish or reward people for each of their deeds; therefore, it is useless to blame him. The actions of each person, right or wrong, have inevitable developments that result from their own choices and decisions. You are, therefore, solely responsible for your deeds.

Cause & Effect

To understand what the word consequence means, we must match it to a scientific theory called "Cause and Effect" or the concept of causality, which refers to the relationship between a cause and an effect. This is the principle by which one thing results directly from another. According to this theory, every consequence has a source. Causation is the "why" of things. The effect is the sequel to the determinant. Thus, when scientists want to understand why such a phenomenon has occurred, they look for the determinant. The cause is what induces an effect and explains it. Science says that life is always in motion, and this perpetual motion is generated by the causes and effects that follow one another in an endless temporal succession.

The universe is a system of relationships where things in themselves are less important than the relationships that govern them. Causality is the principle that governs the links between causes and effects, on the one hand, and actions and consequences. Causality determines that what's happening now is the sequel of what happened the moment before.

Acts and Consequences

Acts and consequences are to spirituality what cause and effect are to science. The causal implications are, in both cases, necessary to understand a sequel or a reaction. Without reason, there is no effect, and without an act, there is no consequence. To find out why something happened, one must know what induced it to happen. However, the comparison stops there, because acts and consequences differ significantly from causes and effects. All existing things can be a cause because everything that exists has a purpose since God did not create anything that has no use. The causes and effects are in the realm of physics, whereas consequences are purely anthropic and moral, they relate to the activity and spirituality of man.

When the consequence is remote from the action that caused it, some call it the fruit, for they need longer to mature before they come up. After sowing a seed, for instance, it takes a while before a plant can be harvested.

Causes produce effects, whereas acts produce consequences, for they are induced by an intent. Consequences are not to be confused with divine reprimands or sanctions imposed by God for a wrong decision; they are only the sequel of an act. These outcomes are not due to fate or chance.

Motivation—Volition—Intention

Spiritual deeds must be intentional and motivated to produce consequences rather than mere effects. It would, therefore, be more accurate to say that deliberate and motivated actions have consequences. Effectively, intents not followed by action do not produce significant results; and isolated, unintentional, and unmotivated actions can have only minor effects.

Motivation assigns goals to acts. The engine propels an

Ignore them and bear the consequences

action towards achieving a goal. The intention is an inclination to accomplish a particular purpose, and it is a prerequisite in the decision-making process. Intent gives its specificity and value to the act. Motivation and purpose characterize an act.

The intention is a project nurtured internally, waiting for when the time comes to be activated. This is what lawyers call premeditation. The moral of intent is that in the determination dwells the sin, and it is, therefore, to the purpose that the consequence is attached. The intention is, therefore, inseparable from the deed. It is sometimes the dominant element of the act. The action itself could even remain unaccomplished, and in such a case, the intention could be as wrong as the action itself could have been.

The righteousness of the voluntary intention that motivates the act has beneficial consequences. If, before acting, you reflect on the possible outcomes, and if you are sure of the righteousness of your intention, your deed will be filled with the Spirit of God. However, justifying a wrongful action by evoking the legitimacy of its end would have negative consequences, for, in the ethics of spirituality, the purposes do not validate the means.

Voluntary actions imply that their authors know well what they are doing; they know that their actions would produce consequences, even if they ignore the seriousness, the extent, and the nature of these consequences. They must, therefore, accept responsibility for the consequences of their actions because they acted on their own free will. If someone knows a decision he is about to make is illegal and makes it all the same, then they accept the risks and must bear the consequences.

Volition, in free will, implies that since you have the freedom to act and you freely make up your mind and decide based on your own will you will bear all the consequences of your deed. Free will is said to be the mother of all unfavorable outcomes.

It is essential to think about the action before undertaking it, to benefit from an experience of life, because, in the great river of life, finding past actions and their associated consequences is an impossible task.

Volition condones an action. It is the desire to do something voluntarily and on your own free will, towards reaching a goal. Motivation associated with self-determination and intention is the condition for the consequences of an action to be attributable to you.

Other People's Deeds?

Like most people, you may think that the consequences of your actions cannot affect others since the links between your decisions and other peoples are not noticeable. However, if you acknowledge that your actions influence the course of the river of your life, you also must agree that the existence and future of others are also affected. The reverse is true. The consequences of the actions of a man are, as a natural phenomenon, subject to the influence of a variety of external causes. All the implications of human deeds are linked and determined by the endless succession of consequences and effects. The present state of your consciousness is the consequence of its former state, and it causes the one that will follow.

All life experiences result from previous actions, although your reactions to these experiences are not predetermined. Each of your responses is an action that will generate its own consequences. Wrong decisions create situations conducive to further flawed choices. Whatever the motives behind your choices and decisions, you always have the option of making the appropriate decision.

You are, yourself, the cause of the consequences you will produce throughout your life. You are responsible for your

Ignore them and bear the consequences

choices and behaviors, and you must accept the results of your decisions, actions, words you uttered, and thoughts you have spread throughout your life. No one can prevent acts from producing consequences. Choices and outcomes are inextricably linked, as the two faces of a coin. None of the correlates can exist without the other.

Now that you have familiarized yourself with those basic concepts and definitions, let's see what the Bible teaches about some of the sternest consequences.

Salvation and Eternal Life

Salvation is a consequence of the choices and of the deeds of your entire life. Salvation is not determined by how you observe the divine commandments; how you abide by the rules of ethical conduct; how you say your daily prayers and devotions; by the purity of your soul, or for showing up punctually at church on Sundays. Salvation is determined by the consequences of your choices and of the deeds you have done, day after day, during your entire life.

You already know those who call on the name of God will be saved, and whoever invokes his name will be granted eternal life. The Bible says, however, how could anyone hope to be delivered from all their sins if they don't invoke the name of God? "Whoever shall call on the name of the Lord shall be delivered" (Jl 2:32, Acts 2:21b, Rom 10:13). In these verses, the word "whoever" doesn't leave room to doubt or to another interpretation. Those who believe in him, whoever they may be and wherever they come from, may call upon his name, for whoever invokes his name will be granted salvation. The divine promise is immutable and universal. It is not exclusive to a particular group. God made this promise to all his children. Does a good father favor some of his children to the detriment of the others?

To this merciful promise, God has placed only a modest condition: He wants you to invoke his name. If you do not know how to ensure your redemption, just call on his name! God has pledged to keep his promise, and he always keeps his promises. Invoke his name, and you will be saved. Invoke another name than God's, and, as a consequence, you might sink into eternal oblivion. Ignore the divine requirement to invoke his name, and you will bear the consequences, for God grants salvation to those who call on his name.

Being Heard of God

The Bible says: Hold God's Will in contempt, and He might turn His back on you. "The Lord is with you, while ye be with him; and if ye seek him, he will be found of you; but if ye forsake him, he will forsake you." (2 Chr 15: 2) But, some might say, I thought God never forsakes us! "I will never leave thee, nor forsake thee." (Heb 13: 5). Besides, how could God forget His children, whom He loves so much? "When my father and my mother forsake me, then the Lord will take me up." (Ps 27:10).

Two other biblical verses say something about this. "We are troubled on every side, yet not distressed; we are perplexed, but not in despair; Persecuted, but not forsaken; cast down, but not destroyed" (2 Cor 4:8–9). "In all their affliction he was afflicted, and the angel of his presence saved them: in his love and in his pity he redeemed them; and he bare them, and carried them all the days of old." (Is 63:9) These verses are complementary. 2 Cor 4:8–9 says that you may be in distress, but not abandoned to despair, God can turn His back on you, but not leave you to your fate, for God does not forsake his children.

When the Lord told Moses that his death was near, he also

Ignore them and bear the consequences

revealed how his people would behave after his death. They will return to their ancient idols. And the Lord said unto Moses, "They will forsake me, and will break my covenant" (Dt 31:16). Then the Lord revealed to Moses how he intended to deal with the rebellious people. The Lord said, "I will forsake them, and I will hide my face from them" (Dt 31:17); And, in the same verse "Many evils and troubles shall befall them"; And finally, again in the same verse, the Lord revealed that all these measures were not punishments against His people and that He did not intend to abandon them. God's only intent was to help his people find the right way by themselves, and, he added, "So that they will say in that day, are not these evils come upon us, because our God is not among us?" (Dt 31:17).

Invoke God, and He will move toward you, and help you find Him. The Scripture says: "The Lord thy God, he it is that doth go with thee; he will not fail thee, nor forsake thee." (Dt 31:6). Ignore God, and He will turn His back on you, He will hide His face from you, and you won't see the image of His reassuring presence. He will not disappear from your life, but He will not make Himself easily found by you, and you will not know the joy of beholding the image of His presence. Your existence may simply become harder. Evils and afflictions might permeate your life and impact your prosperity. "Ye cannot prosper? because ye have forsaken the Lord, he hath also forsaken you." (2 Chr 24:20).

Not Being Heard by God

If you don't invoke God or you call on any god other than the Lord your God, you should not be surprised if your supplications are not heard. Your requests will remain outstanding. You will find at your expense that no one can live without a little help from God. In times of uncertainty and trial, your cries will resound in the void like the echo that the mountains send back. It will be hard for you to find him and ask him to hear your supplications. The Bible says. "I also will laugh at your calamity; I will mock when your fear cometh; When your fear cometh as desolation, and your destruction cometh as a whirlwind; when distress and anguish cometh upon you. Then shall they call upon me, but I will not answer; they shall seek me early, but they shall not find me." (Prv 1:26–28).

Renouncing God's Forgiveness

Don't invoke the name of God, and risk forgoing God's mercy. God's mercy is like an emergency security exit never closed to who experiences the burning feeling of remorse. The Scripture reveals that the Lord forgives all our iniquities. "Who forgiveth all thine iniquities; who healeth all thy diseases" (Ps 103: 3) Repentance, confession, reparation, and atonement are but hollow words without the hope of divine forgiveness.

Whoever renounces divine forgiveness also takes the risk of no longer knowing how to love. The Scripture says: "To whom little is forgiven, the same loveth little." (Lk 7:47). You may think that one can well live without being loved; the selfish and ego centrists care little about being loved; But what about you, could you live without love? This is not possible for a spiritual being.

He who does not invoke the Lord does not know how to love, and cannot come close enough to God to know Him, says the Bible.

"He that loveth not knoweth not God; for God is love." (1 Jn 4:8).

Renouncing God's Grace

Whether by indifference, contempt, or lack of good judgment, those who shun God's grace will not be loved by him. The LORD said, "I love those who love me" (Prv 8:17); And the Bible says, "You shall love the LORD your God with all your heart and with all your soul, that you may live." (Dt 30: 6, Mt 22:37, Mk 12:30, Lk 10:27). However, God is merciful; he always leaves a door open to those who want to be reconciled with him. "Come back, rebellious children, I will forgive your unfaithfulness." (Jer 16:20)

Esau shunned God's grace, and it was a wrong decision, for he had to endure the consequences of his deed. Rebecca, Isaac's wife, bore twins. Esau was born first, quickly followed by Jacob. Esau became a tall fellow who loved life in the open air and hunting.

Jacob was of a different character. It is said of him he spent more time in his tent, thinking and discussing with others than in the open air. Isaac was fond of Esau, his eldest son, for he was a good hunter, and he often brought him venison, which he liked very much.

Rebecca had a thing for her second son, Jacob. She always pushed him to act as if he were the eldest of the two brothers, although this privilege belonged right to Esau, the firstborn. Encouraged by his mother Rebecca, Jacob obtained the blessing of his father, Isaac, through a subterfuge. Jacob disguised himself to look like his brother Esau and Isaac, who was blind, believing he was dealing with Esau, gave him his blessing.

Esau loudly expressed his dissatisfaction. The Bible says. "He [Jacob] hath supplanted me these two times: he took away my birthright; and, behold, now he hath taken away my blessing." (Gn 27:36) This action seemed very objectionable, and some blamed Jacob for this gesture. But was it really? Did Jacob steal Esau's birthright?

Esau seems to forget that he, himself, sold his birthright to Jacob for the price of a lentil dish. How disdainful he was towards his legacy. When Jacob asked him to sell him his birthright, which he did not know what to do with, Esau even made this scornful remark, "What profit shall this birthright do to me?" (Gn 25:32). The Bible says. "Thus Esau despised his birthright" (Gn 25:34). When he accuses his brother of having taken away his birthright, Esau does not tell the truth.

Jacob only took what his brother had rejected with contempt. Esau still wanted to receive the blessing of his father, but not the duties and responsibilities inherent to birthright. However, birthright is a divine blessing, and nonetheless, Esau despised it; therefore, Esau should bear the consequences of his deed.

Don't forget that it was at the insistence of his mother, that Jacob used this ploy. Did Rebecca act wrongfully? Why did she do that? Well, Rebecca did so because God had announced it to her and she wanted God's Will to be accomplished.

The Bible says, "The elder shall serve the younger" (Gn 25:23), so Jacob would assume the succession and the duties that God had given to Abraham, who transmitted it to Isaac.

From now on, Jacob will have the honor and responsibility to lead his people to the land that God had promised to Abraham and his people.

Thus, the Divine Will is fulfilled. Esau having ethical renounced divine grace, he could no longer fulfill the Will of God as announced to Rebecca, and the convoluted paths taken by Jacob and Rebecca had no other goal than to fulfill the Will of God.

Ignore them and bear the consequences

Forgoing God's Love

To invoke God's name is to show you love him. Fail to invoke his name and renounce the love that God generously gives to those who call on him. The Scripture says, "And we have known and believed the love that God hath to us. God is love; and he that dwelleth in love dwelleth in God, and God in him. God is love; And he that abideth in love dwelleth in God, and God dwelleth in him." (1 Jn 4:16).

Whether through indifference, negligence, contempt, or lack of faith, those who choose not to love God will not be loved by him. The Lord said, "I love them that love me; and those that seek me early shall find me." (Prv 8:17). And the Bible says, "Love the Lord thy God with all thine heart, and with all thy soul, that thou mayest live." (Dt 30: 6, Mt 22:37, Mk 12:30, Lk 10:27).

However, God is merciful; He always leaves a door open to those who want to reconcile with him. The Bible says. "Return, ye backsliding children, and I will heal your backslidings." (Jer 3:22).

Moving God's Mercy Away from You

Some folks invoke God, but sometimes they also allow themselves to invoke occult entities. This is the sign of a faltering or even a non-existent faith. If you believe that other gods exist who will give you what the Lord your God does not want to provide you with, you make a grave mistake, a sin of idolatry and of blasphemy. No one can give you what god is not likely to let you have. You don't have the choice to address your requests either to God or to your favorite idol. The Bible says. "They that observe lying vanities forsake their own mercy." (Jon 2:8).

To those who place their trust in false gods, and who in distress turn again to God, the Lord says, "But where are thy gods that thou hast made thee? let them arise, if they can save thee in the time of thy trouble." (Jer 2:28).

Those who wander thus cannot ignore that he who invokes God will receive everything from him, including the forgiveness and love he generously gives to those who invoke him. The Scripture says, "God shall supply all your need" (Phil 4:19). Those who persist in wandering aimlessly, are they ignorant of what awaits them? The Lord said, "there is no god with me: I kill, and I make alive; I wound, and I heal: neither is there any that can deliver out of my hand." (Dt 32:39).

How do they hope for salvation? False gods, saints, angels, talismans, ventriloquists, nor all the idols of the earth, have the power to grant forgiveness of sins and divine love, without which no one can live; salvation comes from God, and God alone can deliver you from all your sins and save you. The Scripture says, "Whoever shall call on the name of the Lord shall be delivered" (Jl 2:32, Acts 2:21, Rom 10:13).

Those who fail to give to the Lord the love he claims, by exclusively invoking his name will know the throes of multiple physical afflictions. The Bible says, "And thy life shall hang in doubt before thee; and thou shalt fear day and night, and shalt have none assurance of thy life" (Dt 28:66). They will also be tormented by disabling, obsessive, or compulsive mental afflictions. These afflictions will be their new master, and they will find it hard to get rid of them. The Bible says. "The Lord shall smite thee with madness, and blindness, and astonishment of heart" (Dt 28:28)

These disturbances will be recurrent and will disturb the lives of the afflicted; They are similar to some prevalent neurotic afflictions called obsessive-compulsive disorders. Excessive fear of bacteria and the exaggerated mania for hygiene and cleanliness; The unreasonable feelings of insecurity (have I closed all the windows and all the doors?); The insanity of ensuring that objects are always in the same place; The constant presence in the mind of incongruous images and religious thoughts; The obsession of not keeping at bay these blasphemous or obscene thoughts that dwell in your brain; The mania of hoarding various objects; Or those repetitive mental rituals, such as counting aimlessly, or irrationally repeating words or phrases, even though they may come from prayers.

To relieve their anxiety, people who suffer from such disorders abide by superstitious rites, which make them repeat themselves endlessly. They try to ward off fate, to alleviate their fears, and to keep aside the evil powers of which they believe they are the victims. The Scripture says, "Will God hear his cry when trouble cometh upon him?" (Jb 27: 9).

The faith of those suffering from these torments is confused. They privilege the mechanical rituals that neurosis imposes on them, to the sound and reasonable practice of faith, which God demands. The Bible says. "But the hour cometh, and now is, when the true worshippers shall worship the Father in spirit and in truth: for the Father seeketh such to worship him." (Jn 4:23).

Those who wander thus are not without knowing that, should they invoke God, they will receive everything from him, including the forgiveness and love he generously gives to everyone who calls on him. The Scripture says, "God shall supply all your need" (Phil 4:19).

Those who persist in wandering aimlessly, are they so ignorant of what awaits them? The Lord said: "there is no god with me: I kill, and I make alive; I wound, and I heal: neither is there any that can deliver out of my hand." (Dt 32:39). How do they hope for salvation? False gods, saints, angels, talismans, ventriloquists, nor all the idols of the earth, have the power to grant forgiveness of sins and divine love, without which no one can live; salvation comes from God, and God alone can deliver you from all your sins and save you. The Scripture says, "Whoever shall call on the name of the Lord shall be saved" (Jl 2:32, Acts 2:21, Rom 10:13).

However, God is merciful. He does not abandon those who return to him. The Bible says: "He maketh sore, and bindeth up: he woundeth, and his hands make whole." (Jb 5:18) When the sinner has understood and calls on God to heal him, all his afflictions will disappear. The Bible says, "Come, and let us return unto the Lord: for he hath torn, and he will heal us; he hath smitten, and he will bind us up." (Hos 6: 1).

Samuel's first book reveals a dramatic story and its terrible consequences to the people of Israel when they had returned to idolatry. In a confrontation with the Philistines, the Hebrews suffered a severe defeat. They wondered why the Lord had let them lose this battle. Instead of calling upon God, they took the Ark of the Covenant with them into the burning desert. They believed the sacred ark would protect them from their enemy and would assure their victory. Impudently they conferred supernatural powers on the ark, which was only a wooden box containing objects used for worship. They used it as a lucky charm, an idol, in which they put all their trust. They firmly believed that it had the power to save them. They did not even feel the need to call upon God, so much did they trust in this wooden god created by the hand of man. As soon as the ark was among them, the people rejoiced and uttered such shouts of joy that the Philistines became alarmed. The latter were panicked when they saw that the ark had reached the camp of the Hebrews because they thought that the god of Israel had also come to lend a helping hand to the Hebrews. The Philistines feared the god of Israel, for they remembered that he had helped the Hebrews to beat the Egyptians and that he had inflicted terrible wounds upon the mighty armies of Pharaoh. Despite their fears, the Philistines fought and won. Israel was defeated, and the Philistines seized the ark and carried it away as a trophy. The Hebrews lost thirty thousand men in this battle. The two sons of Eli, Hophni, and Phinehas, who had been assigned to protect the ark, perished. When Eli heard the news, he fell from his seat backward, broke his neck, and died. The Hebrews did not recover the ark until seven months later, but not until twenty years later did they finally understand their error and invoked God again. Then Samuel spoke to the people of Israel. "If ye do return unto the Lord with all your hearts, then put away the strange gods and Ashtaroth from among you, and prepare your hearts unto the Lord, and serve him only." (1 Sm 7:3).

"No man can serve two masters: for either he will hate the one, and love the other; or else he will hold to the one, and despise the other. Ye cannot serve God and mammon." (Matthieu 6:24)

Wounds, Aches, and Afflictions

The Bible says: Those still dithering about seeking God and understanding what His will is will live a life of discomfort. They will experience small physical and mental afflictions, which, although not deadly, will make their daily life very uncomfortable. "The wicked shall be filled with mischief." (Prv 12:21). "Innumerable evils have compassed me about: mine iniquities have taken hold upon me" (Ps 40:12).

However, all these evils suffered by men can be deleted without leaving a trace, as the wave erases the footsteps on the sand, for God helps those who seek Him, the Bible says. "They that seek the Lord shall not want any good thing." (Ps 34:10). And: "Without faith it is impossible to please him: for he that cometh to God must believe that he is, and that he is a rewarder of them that diligently seek him." (Heb 11: 6).

Your quest for God and the divine will is your personal effort to learn to know Him, to establish a personal relationship of trust with Him. It is not a destination but a journey, and in this sense, it is the higher act of devotion that a believer can offer to God. Then, when you call upon him, he will hear you, and he will listen to your requests; And when you pass through an ordeal, he will be at your side to bring you solace, as would your best friend.

If you fail to undertake the first step when attempting to seek him, he will always seem distant and unapproachable. Why would he go to you if you have not indicated your strong desire to meet him by initiating the first step? How do you expect him to answer your requests, if he does not know you personally, and if he does not recognize you as a member of his close circle of friends? It is up to you to take the first step towards God. The Scripture says, "Who hath first given to him, and it shall be recompensed unto him again?" (Rom 11:35).

If you are determined to abide by his will, start your personal quest for God immediately; Then, you will go to him to know him better; Then only you will understand who God is, what His will is, and what he wants you to do, the Bible says. "Seek ye me, and ye shall live." (Am 5: 4) But, start immediately, for the Scripture says, "Those that seek me early shall find me." (Prv 8:17).

Saying "No" to the Divine Promise

Seeking God to establish a personal relationship with him is not an option; It is mandatory! If you do not undertake your own quest for God at the earliest, you cannot understand what his will is. You will never know what God wants and what he wants you to do.

Ignore them and bear the consequences

The consequences of this carelessness on your part may be severe. This is the source of all the evils and all the hardship in your life. Nothing is worse than the feeling of never being heard. No one is at your side to comfort you in times of distress; no one to show you the light in times of uncertainty, and no one to fill you with hope when you are hopeless. Quit seeking God, and you will forgo His promise.

The effort needed to seek him is not insurmountable. The Lord said, "Ye shall seek me, and find me, when ye shall search for me with all your heart." (Jer 29:13–14). In the first part of this verse, God reveals what those who seek him will find him: those who seek me will find me; And, in the second part, God announces there is a condition, one only, to his promise: you must seek him with all your heart. Only those who seek God with fervor will find him. For evidently, he will help those who wholeheartedly engage in the quest of God and of the divine will.

Admit that this is not an impossible condition for anyone who wants to find him. God invites you, he keeps his doors wide open for you, and his only request is that you make efforts to search him. Think carefully about this adage, "If you go fishing, you can never be sure you'll catch a fish; But if you do not fish, you can be pretty sure you won't catch one."

In our particular case, the issue is much more critical. The purpose of the divine quest is not to bring home fish, but to find God. In addition, God committed to helping you to discover him, while the fish will do all it can to avoid getting caught by your hook, and you cannot blame it for this.

The Scripture says, "I will be found of [by] you, saith the Lord" (Jer 29:14). So, if you believe it's too hard for you to produce the little effort the Lord requires from you, you must review your judgment.

All those who seek God will find him, for God will make

himself discoverable by all those who try to look for him with all their hearts.

God did not create you to then leave you alone in life, defenseless in the wilderness. God has chosen you, and he granted you the immense privilege of coming to life and stand by him. God needs you. If he elected you, it is because he needed you to help him ensure the continued existence and well-being of his creation and creatures.

No valid excuse exists for those who fail to seek the Lord and to understand what God's will means. Simply, they will not be part of the club. They will not have access to the close circle of God's chosen ones. God will let them live on earth for the rest of the time allotted to them, like sheep in their pens or rats in public dumps. They cannot blame him, and say: He does not hear my supplications! God's promise will be removed from their reach and will become void as for them, the Bible says. "Destruction cometh; and they shall seek peace, and there shall be none." (Ez 7:25).

Good Riddance to Providence

Bees come to mind when the price of fruit and vegetables rises sharply. The increasing use of powerful insecticide causes a high rate of mortality to the familiar honeybees. In the United States, beekeepers lost about 40–44% of their bees for the year ending in spring 2015. Few people can fathom the upcoming catastrophe. Let's imagine the following scenario. You go to your local supermarket, and you see that half of all the shelves are empty. The shelves of fruits, vegetables, dairy products, tea, coffee, chocolate, flowers, and plants have been emptied and cleaned. You ask the cashier whether the shelves will be resupplied soon, for you intend to come back later to make your purchases, and the cashier answers you: no! You take his answer for a joke, and ask: what am I going to do for dinner? The cashier replies: we will receive soon substitute synthetic products with artificial flavors that mimic the taste of vegetables and the fragrance of fresh fruits. It sounds like an unlikely and even absurd sci-fi scenario. However, it could happen, and much sooner than you might think. All the products sold in these departments depend on pollination by bees. Unfortunately, the extensive use of increasingly potent pesticides massively extinguishes bees. Will bees come back someday? No one knows, but one thing is sure, with no bees, food will become rare, for the beasts and for men.

Bees' providential action ensures abundant harvests. God wants each one of his creatures to work for its own profit, and also for the good of all. Although God relies on bees to convey his blessings to us, the benefits are from God, not from the bees. God wants the living beings (plants, animals, and humans) and the inanimate objects he created to depend on each other and to interact in perfect symbiosis. Living particles are interconnected, interacting with one another. But let's go a little further, to understand the interaction between human cells and foreign cells that cooperate to produce mutual benefits. Don't you think that is possible?

You have learned from a very young age how important it is to maintain good hygienic practices, and you wash your hands regularly, fearing bacteria. But don't you know that bacteria are not all harmful? Some are not only useful to humans, but they are indispensable to our well-being. Do you know that 90% of the cells in your body are bacterial cells, foreign cells of non-human origin? Scientists call "microbiota" the mass of bacteria that used to be called "intestinal flora."

The microbiota is an ecosystem with which we live in perfect harmony. These bacteria live predominantly in the intestine and also in the mouth, throat, nose, vagina, digestive tract, and on the skin. Their overall weight varies between 2 to 4 pounds, depending on the hosting bodies. 100,000,000,000,000 (one hundred trillion) bacteria live in the intestine of an average man, like times more than the number of human cells that make a human body; The microbiota is made of over 3 million bacterial genes. It is one hundred and fifty (150) times larger than the total of human genes, which contains only about 20,000 genes. Don't panic; it's not over yet. This massive community of immigrant cells invisible to the naked eye, the microbiota, entertains excellent relationships with our own cells and organs. Between these colonies of foreign cells and our individual cells, a continual flow of peaceful exchanges exists.

Where do all these bacteria come from? The first bacteria are transmitted from the mother to the child at birth. The fetus lives in a sterile environment, but when it can break the placental envelope, the newborn is immediately colonized by its mother's bacteria. 24 hours after birth, it already harbors a healthy colony of one hundred billion (100,000,000,000) bacteria. This initial colony will be later joined by other bacteria coming from the environment or from people with whom the newborn has contacts. At two or three years of age, the microbiota of the infant matures, with a colony of about one hundred trillion (100,000,000,000,000) bacteria.

What are these bacteria used for? They need us as much as we need them. They can only live in our bodies, and mostly in our intestines. Scientists have recently discovered that imbalances in the mix of microbiota bacteria could be responsible for obesity, insulin resistance, diabetes, allergies, depression, and many other diseases.

These bacteria act as highly specialized workers who know how to do things for us that we do not know how to do. They know, for instance, how to synthesize various substances that act as neurotransmitters. Neurotransmitters are used by our bodies to communicate and carry information and instructions between our brain neurons and all of our cells. The microbiota continually interacts with all our cells. It maintains law and order in the colony, so a species of bacteria cannot grow to the point of becoming more potent than the others, and seize power. If a group of bacteria could overpower the others, it could mean serious health problems or even death to the hosting body. If deadly bacteria invade your microbiota to commit a misdeed on your person, they would be held in check by other tribes of friendly bacteria. Without these bacteria, you could not digest certain foods and resist diseases.

Wait, that's not all! The activities of the intestinal microbiota in human metabolism make it an organ in its own right. The microbiota is involved in developing your immune system. It facilitates the metabolism of sugars, proteins, bile acids, dietary fiber, and vitamins. The microbiota deserves to be called an organ, because, like other organs, it produces hormones that act on our brain.

A mere alteration of the bacterial population mix inside the intestine can cause metabolic disorders such as type 2 diabetes, obesity, cardiovascular disease, chronic inflammatory bowel syndrome, allergies, depression, or colorectal cancer.

To conclude, these dear bacteria will not survive you. When God calls you back to him, they will render an ultimate service by helping your mortal remains return worthily to the dust, in fulfillment of the divine will.

Beholding bees, worms, and bacteria's providential actions give a glance at God's complex ways to ensure the everlasting sustainability of the creation.

God requires that everyone contributes actively to the good of all. If God's blessings reach us

through complicated means, through the bee, the earthworm, the bacteria, etc., no doubt exist that God sends his blessings to us.

Disrupting God's seamless organization, or failing to do your part in the functioning of his global creation, might move the Divine Providence away from you.

Being Forgotten by God

False preachers are false prophets, and false teachers, but of a rather peculiar nature. They have in common with some Christians an unfortunate tendency to pronounce divine judgments, which are not issued by God. Let's call them "fake preachers," preachers being those who proclaim the Word of God, it is easy to conclude that he who preaches his own word is a false preacher. Well-intentioned men, spiritual guides, pastors, may sometimes behave like false preachers, even though they have no evil intention, the Bible says. "The anointing which ye have received of Him abideth in you, and ye need not that any man teach you." (1 Jn 2:27).

Many kinds of false preachers live among us. Some are preachers who preach hellfire and damnation. They have a peculiar predilection for talking about hell in their sermons, the smell of sulfur that reigns there permanently. They love to describe the frightening horned demons pushing the unfortunate sinners into the flames with long forks. How often haven't you heard someone say: "this person will go to hell?" Haven't you heard one false preacher describe in great detail what the hell looks like? I must confess that I do not know what the hell is like, for so far, I have never died. I never talked to anyone who had gone to hell after his death and paid me a visit thereafter, to discuss the matter. Such testimony would have been compelling if this person had

Ignore them and bear the consequences

the privilege of visiting hell and survive his experience to tell his story to the rest of us.

These preachers of hellfire and damnation preach their own word, not God's. They do it knowingly or by mere ignorance. The Scripture mentions the Sheol, the kingdom of the dead, a place where the dead sojourn. Sheol is often mistakenly translated by "hell." The word hell appears so rarely in the Bible, with such meager description, that it is hard to know if the biblical authors were speaking of the same thing. Anyway, hell, paradise, afterlife, future, redemption, are hidden things that fall within the reserved domain of God. Those who claim to reveal the hidden things that only God knows are mere impostors, for God alone knows the future. God alone knows who will go to hell, if any. God alone knows what the hell is like if hell exists. Among these preachers of hell and damnation, some excel at a second specialty: preachers of hatred, preachers of lies, preachers of deception, etc.

If you think that you are sufficiently warned against these false preachers and believe they can do no harm to someone like you, you are wrong! False preachers are among us, always ready to announce the message of God, with a talent for persuasion, authority, and charisma, they inspire confidence in the faithful. Neither let men, nor dogmas, nor the precepts created by men, come between you and God in your quest for his will. The clergy and the religious authorities are neither prophets nor messengers of God. The Bible says, "In vain they do worship me, teaching for doctrines the commandments of men." (Mt 15: 9); and Peter and the apostles said, "We ought to obey God rather than men." (Acts 5:29).

Beware of the sweet words pronounced by those who approach you in sheep's clothing; you will not always discern the wolf hiding there. The Scripture says, "Beware of false prophets, which come to you in sheep's clothing, but inwardly they are ravening wolves."

(Mt 7:15). Letting these merchants of hope take you with them, you could break your relationship of trust with the Lord, and, as a consequence, you might wander aimlessly in the labyrinth of life, the Bible says. "Believe not every spirit, but try the spirits whether they are of God: because many false prophets are gone out into the world." (1 Jn 4:1).

In the Bible, Jeremiah reveals what he heard from God: "Then the Lord said unto me, The prophets prophesy lies in my name: I sent them not, neither have I commanded them, neither spake unto them: they prophesy unto you a false vision and divination, and a thing of nought, and the deceit of their heart." (Jer 14:14). Jeremiah also reveals the terrible consequences of those who speak in his name, without having received this mission from God: "Therefore thus saith the Lord concerning the prophets that prophesy in my name, and I sent them not, yet they say, Sword and famine shall not be in this land; By sword and famine shall those prophets be consumed." (Jer 14:15). From this verse, it may be concluded those who might go to hell could be those false preachers who take themselves for God.

The Lord reveals the terrible consequences of false preaching. The Lord said, "Their way shall be unto them as slippery ways in the darkness: they shall be driven on, and fall therein." (Jer 23:12).

The Lord does not love those who speak in his name without having received authority. The Bible says, "Behold, I am against the prophets, saith the Lord, that use their tongues, and say, He saith." (Jer 23:31). What stands before those false prophets is frightening. The Bible says, "I will utterly forget you, and I will forsake you, [...] and cast you out of my presence." (Jer 23:39). If you come to this, conclude that you have failed in your quest for God.

Ignore them and bear the consequences

Salvation or Perdition

To do or not to do his will. To do the will of God, one must first understand what the will of God is. You must understand how God hands out his gifts, and you must also understand the divine Providence. God's will, Law # 2, explains what the Bible reveals about the will of God and about Providence. But why is it so essential to work relentlessly to fulfill his will? You may be wondering whether you might face the consequences of living a life with no concern about God's Will. Do you believe that you have always walked in the way of God, although you have probably always privileged your own will? Perhaps, have you relied on the teachings of pious peoples in whom you placed all your trust? Christ said, "Enter ye in at the strait gate: for wide is the gate, and broad is the way, that leadeth to destruction, and many there be which go in thereat: because strait is the gate, and narrow is the way, which leadeth unto life, and few there be that find it." (Mt 7:13–14).

To fulfill the will of God is to work for the redemption of your sins, and to deserve salvation and eternal life; You must ensure you will be saved, for not all are saved. Christ said, "Not everyone that saith unto me, Lord, Lord, shall enter into the kingdom of heaven; but he that doeth the will of my Father which is in heaven." (Mt 7:21). In this verse, Christ reveals that it is not enough to repeat: "Lord, Lord!" to secure a place in paradise; But what you must do above all is the will of the Father; Not the will of men, but the will of God; Not your own will but the will of God. In these two verses, Christ teaches that on the day of judgment, many of his followers will go to him to plead their case. They will call Him Lord, Lord! They will talk about their meritorious works, but he will drive them away, and they will hear from his mouth what no one wants to hear on the day of judgment: go, unholy, you who have never accomplished God's will! Jesus said, "Many will say to me in that day, Lord, Lord, have we not prophesied in thy name? and in thy name have cast out devils? and in thy name done many wonderful works? And then will I profess unto them, I never knew you: depart from me, ye that work iniquity." (Mt 7:22–23).

Eternal salvation, liberating redemption, are no longer negotiable on the day of the Last Judgment. That day you can only hear the verdict of your judges, which will be summed up in one word; saved or lost. This verdict is final and not appealable. Late regrets will have no effect.

Salvation is the struggle of a lifetime. It begins early in youth, and, on the day of judgment will be summed up in a simple question: have you, during your lifetime, worked for fulfilling God's will? Followed by a verdict summed up in one word: saved or lost!

The Pit You Dug

Life is a succession of choices, and each option determines an act. Acts generate reactions, good or bad, which are called consequences. Thus, goes life, like a three-count waltz: several options are available to you, and you must choose one of them; Then you act according to your choice; At a later time, you receive the fruit of your decision and acts. This mechanism repeats itself restlessly, at every moment of your life, both for innocuous decisions and essential choices, and that's how you shape your personality and your future.

What you have become today is the sum of all your

choices and actions, from birth to this day. You are what you have sown throughout your life.

In a very expressive verse, the Bible says, "They have sown the wind, and they shall reap the whirlwind" (Hos 8:7). When you choose, right or wrong, you also determine the nature of the consequence you'll face, favorable or detrimental. If you do not think about the potential future implications of your decisions beforehand, you might regret it; And the reverse is true; The right choices are the guarantors of a pleasant future. It is a divine law that scientists call the law of cause and effect. This principle can easily be verified by another biblical precept. The Bible says, "Speak to the earth, and it shall teach thee." (Jb 12:8). What would the earth say? It would say that if you sow a single grain of wheat, you will harvest an ear containing tens or even hundreds of grains. This means that whatever you do today, good or evil, you will receive the fruit of your acts when the time to harvest comes; you will receive it a hundredfold. The Bible says, "Isaac sowed in that land, and received in the same year an hundredfold" (Gn 26:12).

This law, like all divine laws, applies universally to the whole universe. God's laws are immutable, universal, and eternal, as is God's Will; thus, for instance, no one can be immune from the Divine Law of gravity. Throw a stone to the sky, and it will infallibly fall back upon your head or that of an unfortunate passerby. But who would want to be shielded from this law of the harvest? It gives you assurance that you will collect tens or even hundreds of times what you have sowed, with God's help and a little work on your part? The Bible says: "Be not deceived; God is not mocked: for whatsoever a man soweth, that shall he also reap." (Gal 6: 7).

To mock God means to turn your back on him; It

means you believe you can thwart God's will; it also means you think you are immune from the Lord's laws. However, all this is only an illusion.

Knowing you will reap what you sowed may be a comforting thought, provided you have planted good grain only throughout your life. If such is not the case, and if in your lifetime you ever sowed bad grain, your prospects at harvest time might be less reassuring or even terrifying. It is impossible to sow thistle and hope to harvest oranges.

Who sows hatred and contempt will reap discord; Who sows the love of neighbors shall reap the peace and blessing of the Lord; Who sows ignorance will reap nothingness; Who sows the truth will gain wisdom and respect.

Those who treat the Lord and God's Word with contempt should not hope to receive his gifts and his blessings. What you sow, you will get, do not deceive yourself: you will get a hundredfold what you sowed.

In the parable of the sower, Christ said, "he that received seed into the good ground is he that heareth the word, and understandeth it; which also beareth fruit, and bringeth forth, some an hundredfold, some sixty, some thirty." (Mt 13:23).

Because harvesting always occurs long after sowing, some find it hard to see the cause and effect relationship between sowing and reaping. After planting evil and perceiving no immediate adverse reaction to their act, those who sowed evil might continue to do so. When the time to harvest comes, they will fall under the weight of their crops, the fruit of their evil acts, and their terrifying consequences.

You, yourself, are the happy consequence of your parent's

decision to extend their family. The same holds true for farmers, and for parents, they must wait months before they receive the fruit of their labor. Scientists call this period gestation, farmers talk about maturation, and the Bible speaks of the divine blessing: "and the Lord blessed him." (Gn 26:12). You do not harvest what you just sowed; Harvests take place later, after God has blessed the earth, and this waiting time varies according to species. In the same way, it is impossible to know, at the time of sowing, what the harvests will give, says the Bible. "Sow to yourselves in righteousness, reap in mercy." (Hos 10:12).

He who lives beside God's law will bear the consequences. No one can express contempt for God and escape unharmed, the Bible says. "He that diggeth a pit shall fall into it." (Ps 7:15, 57: 6, Prv 26:27, Eccl 10: 8).

Forgoing an Encounter with God

Loving your neighbor is to love God; not loving your neighbor means not loving God. But to love God, you must know him, for one can only love whom he knows well. To know God, you must be holy, not holy like God, for God's holiness is absolute perfection that no human can equal, but as hallowed as men can be, which means sanctified. The Bible teaches us that to be hallowed as men can be, you must love God, and you must love your neighbor.

Lv 19 reveals two fundamental precepts, the requirement of holiness, "Ye shall be holy: for I the Lord your God am holy." (Lv 19: 2), and the prerequisite to loving your neighbor, "Thou shalt love thy neighbour as thyself" (Lv 19:18).

These two precepts are of the essence in the Old Testament and in the New Testament. The Bible says, "Thou shalt love the Lord thy God with all thine heart, and with all thy soul, and with all thy might." (Dt 6:5, 10:12, 11:13, 30:6); "Thou shalt love thy neighbor as thyself" (Lv 19:18); And Christ said, "Thou shalt love the Lord thy God with all thy heart, with all thy soul, with all thy strength, and with all thy mind; And thy neighbor as thyself." (Lk 10:27, Mt 22:37, Mk 12:30). Fail to abide by these two divine decrees, and you will risk forgoing an encounter with God.

You need to meet with God, to know Him, to better understand His will, to establish a personal and lasting relationship with Him, and to tell Him that you are eager to serve Him. If you find yourself in such a situation where you are unable to faithfully express your love for God and for your neighbor, it means you failed miserably in your quest for God, and your supplications will be more distant and inaudible to the Lord.

The Empty House

In the parable of the empty house, a man's soul is inhabited by evil. Jesus allegorizes this poor man's soul with the image of a poorly maintained home. As soon as the spirit of evil was cast out, the house became clean and tidy. After leaving the mind of this man, the evil spirit wandered in arid and inhospitable lands, looking for a place where he could rest. But, as it did not find it, it said to itself, "I'm going back to this house I left." When it returned, it found that the house was clean and tidy. It then walked away and came back with seven other evil spirits, even worse than himself. Together, they settle in the house and dwell in it. This man's situation was worse than it had been at the beginning, the Bible says. "When the unclean spirit is gone out of a man, he walketh through dry places, seeking rest; and finding none, he knows, I will return to my house whence I came out.

Ignore them and bear the consequences

And when he cometh, he findeth it swept and garnished. Then goeth he, and taketh to him seven other spirits more wicked than himself; and they enter, and dwell there: and the last state of man is worse than the first." (Lk 11:24–26, Mt 12:43–45).

The Parable of the Empty House

The house we are talking about here is actually the spirit of a man. The Bible says, "Know ye not that ye are the temple of God, and that the Spirit of God dwelleth in you?" (1 Cor 3:16). In this verse, the spirit of men is a temple in which the spirit of God dwells. The Scripture often uses the expression House of God. But one may wonder why the evil spirits could so quickly reoccupy the mind of this person, encountering no resistance, any opposition of any kind, while the 'House', that is to say the soul of this man was at last rid of the evil spirit that dwelt in him, and that it now resembled a clean and tidy house. It is easy to understand that if the evil had occupied this house in the first place, it was because it was poorly maintained, abandoned, and, perhaps, hideous in appearance, so the Spirit of God could never stay there. When the evil spirit returned, it found the house empty; the man's mind was empty and without activity. The demon, therefore, hastened to occupy it forcibly, along with other demons of his kind, so nobody could easily cast them out.

The message of this parable of Christ becomes evident.

Do not let your mind empty and fallow, because it is in vacant places that the evil spirits like to dwell. Like hermit crabs, the demon lives in shells that others have discarded. If you drive it away, it will come back forcefully and will reclaim possession of your mind.

Your inner temple that houses the Spirit of God will become the legitimate abode of the devil. The Bible says, "Thy word have I hid in mine heart, that I might not sin against thee." (Ps 119: 11). Who would dare to hide the Word of God and his commandments in the abode of the devil? Would you protect your valuables in a trash can? Isn't this a sufficient reason not to let the evil spirit invade this holy place?

Leave Not Your Mind Lie Fallow

The Apostle Paul teaches us to observe a precept based on two principles. Make sure that the House of God inside of you is never empty and always active. Paul teaches that everyone must be filled with the Spirit of God, and in all circumstances. The Bible says, "Be filled with the Spirit" (Eph 5:18). A man's spirit filled with the Spirit of God is likely to prevent any attempt made by an evil spirit to occupy the place, and it will keep the evil one at bay. During his second trip to Asia Minor, Paul had an encounter with the Bereans, a passionate Jewish community living in the city of Berea in Macedonia, in northern Greece. He noted that the attitude of the Bereans differed significantly from that of other communities he had encountered. The Bereans warmly welcomed Paul and Silas, not because they already knew Paul's message and wanted to hear it from him, not because they were merely curious, but because they did not know him, and they would like to know him and listen to what he had to say. This attitude seduced Paul, do not reject someone with something to say, even if this person does not belong to your community or your church. Instead, show him you are interested in hearing what he has to say. Every word deserves to be heard. Especially since the Bereans did not content themselves with listening passively. They were trained at studying what they heard or what they read.

Ignore them and bear the consequences

They would make sure those words were not contradicting the Scripture, the inspired word of God.

This second characteristic of the Bereans seduced Paul, studying what they heard or what they read and match it with the Scriptures to make sure that it followed the Word of God. Paul integrated it into his teaching, do not reject what you learned without having studied and experienced it. The Bible says, "Prove all things; hold fast that which is good." (1 Thes 5:21). Every upright word deserves to be heard, but it is important to always refer to the Scripture, to make sure that nothing in this word comes in contradiction with the Divine Word.

The experience of Paul and Silas is narrated in Acts 17:10–15, the Bible says. "These [the Bereans] were more noble than those in Thessalonica, in which they received the word with all readiness of mind, and searched the scriptures daily, whether those things were so." (Acts 17:11).

Although Paul did not get the results he expected, because the Bereans had listened to him with the highest interest, but had not accepted his message, for they had to debate between themselves and especially check every word, every idea hidden behind Paul's words, and match them with the Scriptures.

So, Paul's message—we must be filled with the Spirit of God, and we must verify everything we hear and everything we read, to ensure relevance with the divine word. We must not fear to make a mistake; error is not a sin. The absence of error is a sign of emptiness and of lack of activity, the Bible says. "That we henceforth be no more children, tossed to and fro, and carried about with every wind of doctrine, by the sleight of men, and cunning craftiness, whereby they lie in wait to deceive" (Eph 4:14)

The Fruit of the Spirit

The Scriptures should not be read with curiosity as the sole motivation, but on the contrary, they must be studied diligently to understand the divine message and to establish and maintain a close bond with God.

Faith without a mindful spirit is hardly better than superstition, which ignores the Spirit of God. The superstitious don't even try to understand; they believe in their nonsense.

It is the Spirit that allows the development of spirituality in men. Anyone who doubts but persists in wanting to understand is better than the believers who do not know doubt but who exempt themselves from searching and understanding. This is the fruit of the Spirit, the fruit you harvest after you sowed healthy seeds and lovingly nurtured them until, with the Divine Blessing, you reap beautiful fruit.

God put in you a tiny part of his Spirit, take care of it, make it sprout, watch it grow, and collect the delicious fruit it will one day produce, a fruit of love, joy, peace, long-suffering, gentleness, goodness and faith in God, the Bible says. "The fruit of the Spirit is love, joy, peace, long-suffering, gentleness, goodness, faith" (Gal 5:22).

The Word and the Spirit

The divine spirit you must be filled with is essential to understanding the Divine Word. Without Spirit, the Word of God would only be empty text. The reciprocal is also true, without the Word, the Spirit would be purposeless, it would return to square one, not knowing where to go from there, for without a guide, like the first man who had to learn everything through accumulation of errors, at the price of losing paradise, which we strive, today, to find again.

Ignore them and bear the consequences

Tables

Abbreviations (OT)

Book	Short	Book	Short
Amos	Am	Judges	Jgs
1 Chronicles	1 Chr	1 Kings	1 Kgs
2 Chronicles	2 Chr	2 Kings	2 Kgs
Daniel	Dn	Lamentations	Lam
Deuteronomy	Dt	Leviticus	Lv
Ecclesiastes	Eccl	Malachi	Mal
Esther	Est	Micah	Mi
Exodus	Ex	Nahum	Na
Ezekiel	Ez	Nehemiah	Neh
Ezra	Ezr	Numbers	Nm
Genesis	Gn	Obadiah	Ob
Habakkuk	Hb	Proverbs	Prv
Haggai	Hg	Psalms	Ps
Hosea	Hos	Ruth	Ru
Isaiah	Is	1 Samuel	1 Sm
Jeremiah	Jer	2 Samuel	2 Sm
Job	Jb	Song of Songs	Sg
Joel	Jl	Zechariah	Zec
Jonah	Jon	Zephaniah	Zep
Joshua	Jo		

Abbreviations (NT)

Book	Short
Acts of the Apostles	Acts
Apocalypse / Revelation	Rev
Colossians	Col
1 Corinthians	1 Cor
2 Corinthians	2 Cor
Ephesians	Eph
Galatians	Gal
Hebrews	Heb
James	Jas
John (Gospel)	Jn
1 John (Epistle)	1 Jn
2 John (Epistle)	2 Jn
3 John (Epistle)	3 Jn
Jude	Jude
Luke	Lk
Mark	Mk
Matthew	Mt
1 Peter	1 Pt
2 Peter	2 Pt
Philemon	Phlm
Philippians	Phil
Romans	Rom
1 Thessalonians	1 Thes
2 Thessalonians	2 Thes
1 Timothy	1 Tim
2 Timothy	2 Tim
Titus	Ti

www.ingramcontent.com/pod-product-compliance
Lightning Source LLC
LaVergne TN
LVHW091250080426
835510LV00007B/194